MUSIC THERAPY IN A
MULTICULTURAL CONTEXT

of related interest

Creative DBT Activities Using Music
Interventions for Enhancing Engagement and Effectiveness in Therapy
Deborah Spiegel with Suzanne Makary and Lauren Bonavitacola
ISBN 978 1 78775 180 4
eISBN 978 1 78775 182 8

Creative Arts Therapies and the LGBTQ Community
Theory and Practice
Edited by Briana MacWilliam, Brian T. Harris,
Dana George Trottier, and Kristin Long
ISBN 978 1 78592 796 6
eISBN 978 1 78450 802 9

A Comprehensive Guide to Music Therapy, 2nd Edition
Theory, Clinical Practice, Research and Training
Edited by Stine Lindahl Jacobsen, Inge Nygaard Pedersen, Lars Ole Bonde
Foreword by Helen Odell-Miller
ISBN 978 1 78592 427 9
eISBN 978 1 78450 793 0

Tales from the Music Therapy Room
Creative Connections
Edited by Claire Molyneux
Foreword by Sarah Hoskyns
ISBN 978 1 78592 540 5
eISBN 978 1 78450 933 0

Cultural Perspectives on Mental Wellbeing
Spiritual Interpretations of Symptoms in Medical Practice
Natalie Tobert
Foreword by Michael Cornwall
ISBN 978 1 78592 084 4
eISBN 978 1 78450 345 1

Cultural Competence in the Caring Professions
Kieran O'Hagan
ISBN 978 1 85302 759 8

MUSIC THERAPY IN A MULTICULTURAL CONTEXT

A HANDBOOK FOR MUSIC THERAPY STUDENTS AND PROFESSIONALS

EDITED BY
MELITA BELGRAVE AND **SEUNG-A KIM**

Jessica Kingsley Publishers
London and Philadelphia

First published in 2021
by Jessica Kingsley Publishers
73 Collier Street
London N1 9BE, UK

www.jkp.com

Copyright © Jessica Kingsley Publishers 2021
Chapter 2 copyright © Kamica King 2021

Library of Congress Cataloging in Publication Data
A CIP catalog record for this book is available from the Library of Congress

British Library Cataloguing in Publication Data
A CIP catalogue record for this book is available from the British Library

ISBN 978 1 78592 798 0
eISBN 978 1 78450 807 4

Printed and bound in the United States

Contents

Introduction

As a culmination of work through the American Music Therapy Association (AMTA), we are excited to share this textbook *Music Therapy in a Multicultural Context: A Handbook for Music Therapy Students and Professionals*. The editors and primary authors met while serving on the Diversity, Equity, and Inclusion Committee. During our time as a committee we presented regularly and our presentations included status updates on goals and tasks completed by the committee, training sessions, times for the members to discuss issues related to diversity and multiculturalism, and more recently, diversity, equity, and inclusion. At one of the conferences, we were approached by Jessica Kingsley Publishers to create a book on multiculturalism and music therapy. As co-editors, we knew that we wanted to include as many committee members as possible in the project. Thus, we invited authors to each write a chapter on a topic area of interest, through a multicultural lens. Each chapter has a personal story from the author or authors, a literature review on their selected topic, and case scenarios or learning activities that relate to the chapter readings.

Over the years, there has been an increase in research articles, textbook chapters, and textbooks on multiculturalism in music therapy. In our years of teaching music therapy courses at a university, we have found that the existing textbooks do not seem to meet the needs of students and music therapists in their learning of multicultural considerations in music therapy practice and musical culture. Most books cover therapeutic considerations but do not discuss the role of music, culture, and health in music therapy.

We are excited to contribute to the body of literature through this handbook. We believe this book will be unique in the field and can be used in any music therapy course that addresses diversity and culture in therapeutic practice. For example, this text can be used in music therapy foundation/topic courses or practicum classes to address clients' needs, in a psychology of music course to discuss why people respond to music and why music therapy works, and in an introductory music therapy course. In addition, this textbook would be relevant for music therapy labs, world music courses, and other culture and diversity classes. As culture itself is so immense, we have selected some topics in this book that are essential and currently lacking discussions in our field.

This book is very timely, as the profession of music therapy is growing both in the number of practicing music therapists and the number of patients served. In a recent survey conducted by AMTA's Diversity and Multiculturalism Task Force (Kaplan, Belgrave, & Kim, 2014), results showed that music therapists provide services to a very diverse population in terms of ethnicity, religion, gender, sexual orientation, and more. However, most practicing music therapists lack the necessary diversified experiences and effective training. At the same time, university programs in music therapy are accepting more and more diverse students. Our colleagues and many other educators in our field have felt the urgent need to teach the concepts of multiculturalism and diversity but are at a loss as to where to start. Therefore, we believe the text is instrumental for practicing music therapists, educators, clinical supervisors, and students alike.

Other university professors teaching musical therapy courses, as well as clinical supervisors working with students, can read and implement the learning activities and include the text in their music therapy courses. Practicing music therapists can purchase this book to enhance their clinical practice.

Our cultural endeavours constitute a life-long journey. We hope you enjoy our contributions and this book enhances your understanding and skills related to diversity and cultures in music therapy.

Melita Belgrave and Seung-A Kim

Reference

Kaplan, R., Belgrave, M., & Kim, S. A. (2014, November). *The AMTA Diversity Task Force: A Status Report.* Poster session presented at the annual National American Music Therapy Association, Louisville, KY.

CHAPTER 1

Music as an Acculturation Strategy in Culturally Informed Music Therapy

SEUNG-A KIM, PHD, LCAT, MT-BC

Prelude

Culture is all around me. I experience it every day. Everywhere I go, whatever I do, whomever I meet, I experience culture through my own reactions and interactions with people and the environment I am in. I observe how it is deeply embedded in my daily life and how it has evolved and changed over time. To me, culture is fascinating! Culture is deep within us and keeps molding us. Every daily encounter has influenced me to form my own culture. As culture is never constant, my own culture is also dynamic, ever changing by accumulating daily experiences. Therefore, getting in touch with my own cultural heritage is so important because it has been transformed in the past and continues to be transformed in the present. I look forward to witnessing the continued growth of my cultural being.

CASE EXAMPLE

At one culturally informed music therapy (CIMT) session, Youngmi, a middle-aged, well-educated, immigrant woman from South Korea, openly shared her personal problems. Her story began when she came to America 20 years ago and married a Korean immigrant man who was the eldest in his family and responsible for the well-being of his parents and siblings. Living in an extended family has required her to make significant sacrifices. She is obligated to work in her husband's family business. After coming back from work, all the housework and child rearing are her responsibility. Her husband has a dominating presence in the household. The traditional Korean culture always places her interests as a secondary priority. Moreover, her husband maintains a close relationship with his mother, even in adulthood. Thus, the couple's relationship often takes a backseat to the priorities and well-being of the children. Moreover, her children, now all grown-up, do not even understand how their mother has not taken any action regarding this family problem! Over the years, she has felt her identity being consumed by her married life. Consequently, she has developed culture-bound mental health syndromes and, as a result, has had to make many visits to the physician. Youngmi's symptoms are known as *Hwabyeong*, or anger syndrome. The condition of *Han* can also lead to somatic symptoms: "When people die of *Han*, it is called dying of *Hwabyeong*, a disease of frustration and rage following misfortune" (Kim, 1995, p.80). During the CIMT session, Youngmi started to sing a song from a Korean children's cartoon that related to her loneliness, sadness, and endurance.

Study questions

1. What are the presenting problems in this case?

2. What is the symbolic meaning of this song?

3. What are the multicultural considerations?

4. Would you encourage the client to cry during the session or confront the client's family?

5. How would you address *Hwabyeong* or *Han*?

6. Is it the client's responsibility to educate the music therapist about unfamiliar cultural traits?

7. How might a music therapist's own cultural expectations and judgments be manifested in music therapy? Is it a problem if that happens? If it is a problem, how can we address it?

Overview

The role of culture has significant implications for music therapy because culture influences the therapeutic relationship and further affects the whole music therapy process-assessment, treatment, and evaluation (Kim, 2013a; Kim & Elefant, 2016; Kim & Whitehead-Pleaux, 2015): "The role of culture appears particularly important when studying the effects of music on health and well-being: the way we interpret, experience, and react to music is strongly shaped by our personal attributes that are molded by our social and cultural background" (Saarikallio, 2012, p.477).

For example, when working with immigrant clients who come from collectivist societies, the music therapist must understand that extended family members influence important decision making in these societies. To understand cultural identity and group identity, the therapist should be knowledgeable about the history of each group. Otherwise, clients may feel misunderstood by the therapist who comes from a mainstream culture (Kim & Whitehead-Pleaux, 2015).

Culture can be defined as certain shared beliefs, values, worldviews, ideas, artifacts, and styles. The common behavior of the group and its permanence are considered as a specific culture of the group members. In this sense, we are all cultural beings. Multiculturalism means that each group forms its own norms, values, beliefs, and attitudes that are shared by the group members. Each individual belongs to multiple cultural groups. Multiculturalism promotes and respects the existence of various cultures, such as age, gender, ethnicity, race, socio-economic status, affiliations, religions, spiritual practices, and disabilities (Kim & Elefant, 2016; Kim & Whitehead-Pleaux, 2015; Sue & Sue, 2013). This paradigm promotes social justice, liberation, and community empowerment.

As a synthesis of various cultural traits, music has been used as a healing method since preliterate times. Our musical endeavors are naturally cultural, as we have learned them from the culture(s) we belong to. Because music and culture are inseparable and the phenomenon of culture is multilayered and dynamic, culture must be taken into account from the start of the music therapy process.

For music therapists, questions related to culture inevitably come up during clinical and educational practices: What is the role of music within a specific culture? How is music used within that community? How are health and illness viewed in a community? How do I, as a music therapist, affect the clients? How do the clients affect me? How much should the dominant culture be involved in integrating immigrants? Is there any advantage or disadvantage in cross-cultural music therapy? To better understand the role of culture in music therapy, this section examines the characteristics of culture and identifies implications for music therapy.

The characteristics of culture

Complexity

The idea of *culture* has both implicit and explicit meanings. On the one hand, certain behaviors of groups of people are observable (e.g., customs) and are therefore explicit. On the other hand, expectations or hidden norms are regarded as embodying implicit meanings. Developing the concept of implicit meanings rests on the belief that there are principles that regulate the culture, which may be inferred. Therefore, some cultures, or some aspects of culture, are not obvious.

Culture is complex in nature (Berry, 1997). It is difficult to formulate a single perspective about the fundamental nature of culture because culture is never static (Kim & Elefant, 2016; Roland, 1996; Sue & Sue, 2013). Also, within any culture, there is a great deal of individual variation. Culture influences how we assign meanings to a phenomenon. Depending on how we define music and health, a style of music may be considered music to us but not to people from other cultures. Also, the concepts of health and illness are seen differently across cultures (Bruscia, 2014; Spector, 2012). For some within a biomedical model, health and disease are seen in a dualistic way, while for some other cultures, an imbalance between yin and yang causes illness and there is a belief that psychosocial factors promote well-being. In addition, the evaluation of whether a behavior is normal or abnormal depends on social norms. Common symptoms of a disease can be found across cultures, but their expressions may vary.

Therefore, the complexity of culture also plays a role in music therapy (Stige, 2002). For example, the fundamental constructs between individualism and collectivism drastically differ (Beer, 2015; Kim, 2007). If the therapy treatment plans are designed within the orientation of individualism, they may not apply well to clients from a different culture. Without the music therapists' cultural awareness, knowledge, and skills, cultural bias can occur at the initial session and throughout the entire music therapy process (Kim & Whitehead-Pleaux, 2015; Swamy, 2014; Whitehead-Pleaux & Tan, 2017):

> As we are profoundly influenced by the culture surrounding us, much of what we see, hear, and feel is imprinted in our minds. It is through this cultural lens that we view our world. Unfortunately, some of these messages with which we interpret the world contain biases, and we carry them into our sessions with our clients. To practice CIMT, we must embark on a journey of self-exploration to uncover these biases and work through them. (Kim & Whitehead-Pleaux, 2015, pp.59–60)

Music therapy is based on elements that are general to humanity rather than specific to a member of a particular cultural group (Abrams, 2015). Thus, the gap that exists between the therapist and the client is a fundamental, existential gap that exists among all human beings. My direct clinical experience has proven to me the principles expressed above: every therapist, regardless of his or her culture, has to bridge cultural differences that exist between the therapist and the client—in this regard, human insight and understanding have a far greater importance than cultural factors.

This perception of human beings is crucial in the CIMT context and also presents a dilemma. If music therapists focus on their clients as a representative of their cultures only, then it would be hard to understand them as whole beings. Furthermore, if music therapists focus on cultural differences, then it is possible to miss other parts of the clients that do not relate to cultural and historical contexts. Therefore, how can music therapists possibly help the clients as whole persons? Most importantly, can music fulfill a significant role related to cultural divergence and transcend differences between the client and the therapist?

Adaptations need to be made when the music therapist uses methods and instruments originally developed for one group and transfers those to another group (Kim & Whitehead-Pleaux, 2015; Whitehead-Pleaux & Tan, 2017; Vandervoort, 2017). However, cross-cultural transfers and adaptations of music therapy approaches and methods can be problematic. Another option is to develop a new method for the culture that would better fit that specific culture. In his writings, Piaget (1976) stated that creativity and innovative thinking in a given area can often be stimulated by transposing the ideas from a different discipline or context into the situation at hand. In the same way, a music therapist who originates from a culture different from that of the client may be able to transpose musical and other cultural elements into the framework of music therapy.

Theoretical foundations

CIMT (Figure 1.1) is an approach especially designed for clients who have experienced living in two or more cultures. I was born and raised in South Korea, and I came to the United States more than 30 years ago. As an immigrant, I have experienced and witnessed many difficulties in the acculturation process. In the past 23 years of my clinical experience as a bi-cultural music therapist and my experience as an immigrant to the US, CIMT has evolved greatly. Clinically, I have worked with a variety of populations, including both American and Korean-American people who have developmental disabilities, autism, Alzheimer's disease, neurological problems, depression and psychosomatic issues. As I have worked with these populations, I strongly feel that special cultural considerations should be addressed in music therapy.

It is my belief that the need for therapy is a human universal, regardless of the structure of a society and whether it is based on individualism or collectivism. Even in some cultures where therapy is not considered a common or accepted phenomenon, this is not because therapy is not needed but that community or religious leaders and family members have taken on the role of the therapist. With time, people's roles change so that even those within ethnic populations that are reluctant to share personal issues with outsiders become gradually accepting of the function of psychotherapy, particularly because of its confidential nature.

CIMT has been modeled after Priestley's (1975, 1994) analytical music therapy (AMT), a method that has greatly influenced my work as a music therapist. My belief is that among the current music therapy methods available, AMT is the method that most closely resonates with Korean-American clients, particularly with older, first-generation immigrants. Being in harmony with psychoanalytic thinking seems to be in accord with the Korean spirit. This probably reflects some similarity between the society in which Freud lived and the Confucius-influenced Korean society, because both societies are hierarchical and male dominant (Kim *et al.*, 2012; Kim, 2013b).

In conceptualizing this approach for the specific population with which I worked—Korean immigrant families—I have drawn on analytical music therapy (Priestley, 1975, 1994; Scheiby, 2001, 2013, 2015), community music therapy (Kenny & Stige, 2002; Pavlicevic & Ansdell, 2004; Stige & Aarø, 2012), multicultural counseling and therapy (Pedersen *et al.*, 2016; Sue & Sue, 2013), Bruscia's integral approach (Bruscia, 2014; Lee, 2015), and Kenny's field of play (2006). All have had an important impact on my clinical thinking and development as a culturally informed music therapist. Upon integration of the ideas of these theoretical strains, I have developed a set of beliefs that underlies CIMT. What follows is a description of these theoretical beliefs.

We are cultural beings

Our daily cultural experience has shaped us into who we are today, and we also have shaped the culture. It is reciprocal in nature. Every moment in life is a cultural experience. We construct and reconstruct the meaning of life continually as we accumulate life experiences.

Culture is both universal and relative

Can one's psychological process be similar or different across cultures? To what extent are musical and non-musical behaviors in a specific culture universal or relative? Cultural universalism and relativism are no longer viewed by researchers as a dichotomy. Instead, depending on the range of the continuum, there are four positions: extreme relativism, moderate relativism, moderate universalism, and extreme universalism. Influenced by constructivism, which emphasizes multiple realities existing in our society, multiple realities (Vera & Speight, 2003) can exist and the interpretations may vary. For example, wedding and funerals are a common practice in our society, but they are not really universal in how they are conducted and are thus among the most enduring markers of cultural differences. Depending on the position that music therapists take, we focus on how important external environments affect shared psychological functions as a result of different behaviors or how psychological functions are the results of the interactions between us and the context.

Culture in a context

We live within a context, which affects what a person does, says, decides, believes, and values. In many ways, culture is a "living thing" and always exists within the context of "the situation"—all those factors that collectively affect the people who experience them—including social, biological, physical, psychological, historical, and practical. According to Ruud (1997), culture is "a way of living... Cultural performance is linked to the individual's situatedness, a way of perceiving and giving meaning to the world informed by a certain perspective. And this perspective is rooted in the private life-world of the person" (p.89). This aspect of culture requires that the music therapist see beyond the practices, values, and norms of the client's culture and understand the specific situation that confronts the client.

Music is always played within a context (Stige *et al.*, 2010). In some cultures, music is everyday life. The boundaries of music may not be as distinct as in Western societies. Within a specific culture, musical elements can be defined differently. For example, the meaning of music is different between Venda culture in South Africa and in America. Here in America, music is a performance that may occur at concerts and is distinguished from other art forms; however, in Venda, music is an integration of multiple art forms:

> The embodied communicative function of music forms the foundation of human musical interaction. This embodiment, which ranges from the personal to the communal, from the individual to the cultural directly impacts and regulates what music communicates, why humans use music as a tool of communication and the manner in which people have access to and benefit from any level of musicality. (Stige *et al.*, 2010, p.146)

Furthermore, health means vary (Bruscia, 2014; Spector, 2012). In individualistic societies, physical or mental health is considered separately when discussing health, whereas in collectivistic societies, body, mind, and spirit integration is emphasized and health is meaningful when embracing the concept of social and community health. Therefore, social justice philosophy must be integrated into the music therapy process because "Our concerns about the well-being of oppressed groups and incorporating into the philosophies and professional roles for these individuals are not only merely scholarly endeavors but also 'our ethical and moral obligation'" (Vera & Speight, 2003, p.253).

Cultural beings

Does culture derive from the innate nature of all human beings? Or is culture a specific and individual expression of a particular group of people, with a specific history, at a given time, and in response to particular social, psychological, and environmental conditions? Some scholars have integrated both universality and relativism (Epstein, 1998; Sue & Sue, 2013; Wilber, 1979).

This integration is particularly related to the combination of AMT and multiculturalism. I am aware of the innate conflict between these two philosophical thoughts, but it is my belief that both concepts can co-exist and be interrelated. For example, humans all have emotions (universality) and yet experience and express emotions in a unique way (relativism). Therefore, I embrace both concepts and integrate them as a whole. A traditional Asian saying captures my belief: "All individuals, in many respects, are like no other individuals, like some individuals, and like all other individuals" (Sue & Sue, 2013, p.37). Our cultural identity includes the individual, collective, and universal.

Tripartite development of identity

Sue and Sue (2013) pointed out that people typically believe in either universality or cultural relativism and usually ignore the group or collective component; in particular, "mental health professionals in general have generally focused on either the individual or universal levels of identity, placing less importance on the group level" (p.40). In the tripartite model, there are three levels of personality formation: uniqueness, collective, and universal. This model closely illustrates my understanding of the multiple dimensions of a person's identity, but I see the dynamics of these elements in a slightly different light. My understanding of a cultural being is as follows. Each individual manifests three layers of culture: individual, collective, and universal. The *individual culture* is expressed by the uniqueness of each human being and the myriad of individual differences among people. The *collective culture* is composed of gender, religion, profession, education, and marital status, to name a few elements. People may belong to multiple groups, but some group identities may be more salient. The *universal culture,* which all human beings share, is evident in biological and psychological similarities, as well as common life events such as weddings and funerals.

Figure 1.1 shows the dynamics of how these three layers of culture relate to one another and interact with music and consciousness to produce an ultimate state of cultural well-being. The paragraphs that follow define the various constructs in the diagram.

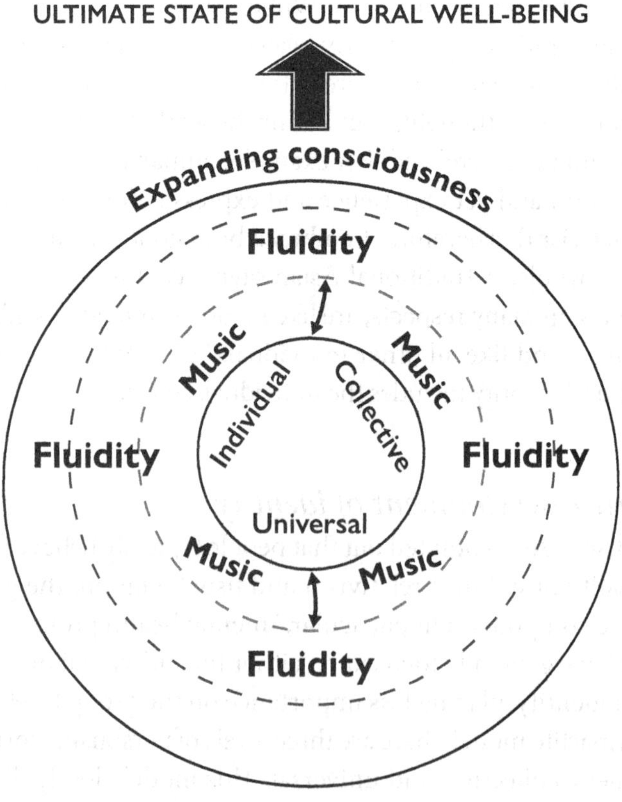

FIGURE 1.1: ULTIMATE STATE OF CULTURAL WELL-BEING

Individual cultural being

Because no one person on Earth is exactly like another, everyone can be understood on his or her own terms and in reference to his or her own self. Depending on life experiences over time, a person's worldview may change. Music therapists accept the fact that every client is unique, which can help avoid making a mistake by overgeneralizing or stereotyping. Each person is a unique individual, so even in a similar situation, the individual's experience and deciphering of meaning is unique. As Bruscia (2000) pointed out, "each person gets completely different samples of experiences, and that each person lives in the implicate order in a different way, because of myriad factors. Thus, throughout the course of life, each person accumulates a unique combination of 'meaning samples'" (p.86).

Collective cultural being

All human beings are innately social beings. Pavlicevic and Ansdell (2004) stated that "we are beings who naturally take part with others and with our surrounding environment" (p.25). The first and fundamental society of human beings is their own family. Every human being is born into a society and belongs to a family as a microcosm of that society. At the very moment we are born, the relationship between at least two human beings begins: we immediately have a mother or primary caretaker. Clients can therefore be understood in that context. As they grow, their social affiliations expand. Each individual collective culture has its own norms and expectations.

The collective nature of identity and the importance of group experience is emphasized by Adler (1959), who states that the essence of normality is having concern for others because human beings have inherent social interest. Isolation, loneliness, and alienation can be unhealthy (Yalom, 1995).

One can strongly feel not only the effect that takes place for clients as individuals but also the effect on an entire group. This can be an experience of healing and bonding for all the members of the group. The energy that can permeate the group can help its members become a community.

Universal cultural being

There are parts of us that are universal. Universality is part of innate human qualities that include universal themes and similarities in humans: "There are some similarities among all *homo sapiens* as a consequence of the biopsychic unity of mankind, and there are further similarities among those who have had more common experiences and face the same sorts of problems" (Swartz & Jordan, 1980, p.158).

Regardless of one's ethnic background, an individual goes through similar life events and emotions. For example, music is a universal phenomenon that people of all ages and cultures experience. Therefore, universality allows us to not feel alone and helps us to "share similar concerns, fantasies, and life experiences with others" (Yalom, 1995, p.41). Yalom suggests that when working with a multicultural group, it is important to emphasize for clients the process of moving away from "cultural difference" toward "transcultural responses to human situations and tragedies that all of us share" (p.7).

Music

Music brings out the growth of our cultural self. Music is used to integrate all three dimensions: the individual, collective, and universal aspects of a person. Using music, we express a way of living, who we are, and where we come from. This is possible because each style of music carries with it a particular framework of reference, just as each individual's lifestyle is unique. Moreover, music has a multi-dimensional energy, which moves us holistically through mind, body, and even spirit. When we listen to music, our body often starts to move, our mind is drawn into the music, and sometimes we are deeply touched spiritually. Like culture, music is never static: "like water, it adapts itself instantly to the shape of its container. In a square vessel, it is square; in a circular vessel, it is circular. This is true because of the nature of the element itself" (Hall, 1982, p.41).

A culturally informed music therapist can use diverse cultural music to help a client prepare for living in a divergent modern society. This cultural understanding helps develop the client's life in a richer way. Therefore, we can use the word "differences" in a positive way. Ultimately, music can transcend time and space.

As Aigen (1997) illustrated, "to participate in the culturally and stylistically embedded music is to participate in culture—it is to participate in the attitudes, values, feelings and experiences which define the culture" (p.23). This is what connects humans collectively. Music transcends the limitations of individuals. Regardless of one's cultural identity, people can connect with each other by sharing musical experiences (Blacking, 1995).

The development of cultural identity
Cultural imbalance

We are the sum of our past, present, and future cultures. Our culture is constantly changing with the accumulation of new understandings in behavioral, psychological, emotional, and spiritual domains. When a new understanding is attained, it expands our culture by modifying or adding to already existing understandings. The acculturation process can take place over time. The process may involve changes in worldviews, values, and social and personal relationships with people and environments.

During this process, a cultural conflict between the existing culture and the new culture inevitably occurs (Kim, 2011, 2013c). This causes a great deal of acculturation stress (Berry, 1997; Berry *et al.*, 1987). Depending on the person's attitude and worldview, the level of acculturative stress varies. It is important to manage this stress to be healthy and to develop a healthier stage of one's cultural identity.

Fluidity of consciousness

Bruscia (2000) formulated the concept of *fluidity*: "if we can be fluid in our consciousness, then we have the richest potential for conceiving what is" (p.86). I have come to believe that "fluidity" is an essential quality for cultural well-being. As Bruscia (2000) asserted:

> This lack of it, this rigidity, this inability to move one's consciousness in and around and through human fields of existence is the most *unmusical* way of being in the world. Music is itself fluidity of consciousness made audible. To be *in* the music, or *with* the music

or to be in any relation to the music is the process of being fluid. It is a surrender to whatever will reveal itself from whatever develops in the music and our experience of it. (p.91)

A person who encounters a new culture and integrates it as part of himself or herself needs to be fluid between the two cultures. To fully integrate the new culture and enjoy it, the first step is to redefine each culture and resolve cultural conflicts. This can only be done by the fluidity of one's consciousness. These layers will be in balance, continuously interrelated, and in touch with one another when a person is in a state of fluidity.

Expanded consciousness

When the three layers of cultural beings are actively interrelated, the person's awareness of his or her consciousness can be expanded toward a well-balanced cultural being to some extent. This is a continuum, as people are informed by a new culture daily.

However, if there is an imbalance in these layers, the person can become stuck, rigid, and unhealthy. When one or more of these areas of our cultural entity is not in balance, psychological, emotional, or behavioral problems can result. When people are unaware that their functioning is diminished in one or more of these areas, there are unhealthy psychological consequences. Also, when a person is not willing to take responsibility for his or her life, or experiences a loss of meaning in life, then he or she becomes unhealthy. These feelings are both intrapersonal and interpersonal. When they have experienced unhealthy relationships with others, they become unhealthy and tend to repeat the same unhealthy relationship patterns. It is important, therefore, to keep expanding one's consciousness.

Ultimate state of cultural well-being

Being in between more than two cultures can be overwhelmingly demanding. Integration takes time and effort, and acknowledging limitations is healthy. To reach a state of cultural well-being, the client's fluidity has to be activated in a full circle. Only then will the client achieve a state of playfulness, show concerns for others, be in touch with nature, and have peace of mind. There are various levels of enlightenment that a person can reach.

Therapist qualifications and self-awareness

Music therapists' ethnocentric attitudes, stereotypes, and preconceptions must be explored prior to their practice (Brown, 2002; Bruscia, 2012; Kim & Whitehead-Pleaux, 2015; Whitehead-Pleaux & Tan, 2017), as this greatly influences the therapeutic relationships with their clients. Being flexible and open to people and life is the core value for CIMT.

A culturally informed music therapist works with all dimensions of human existence: individual, collective, and universal. In addition, the understanding of varied worldviews should holistically take place on both cognitive and emotional levels. The therapist should move in and out of theoretical orientations, methods, and worldviews to address the clients' needs. Musically, the therapist should also be "fluid." Concerning music as an expression of one's culture, how can a therapist be culturally empathetic in understanding the clients without this fluidity? As Brusica (2000) explained, the therapist's responsibility is to share their fluidity of consciousness with their clients.

Needless to say, the culturally informed music therapist needs to have sufficient knowledge about music from a variety of cultures and the history of music in a specific context. The ability of the therapist to listen to the music, analyze it, and engage in the session's verbal encounters is critical in identifying culture-related transference and countertransference phenomena that may arise in the sessions.

If the culturally informed music therapist can utilize the client's primary language, it would be beneficial to facilitate the process, although matching cultural backgrounds between the therapist and the client is not necessary. Because one of the goals in music therapy is to facilitate the client's acculturation process, it is even beneficial for the therapist to have a different cultural background.

It is particularly important that culturally informed music therapists acknowledge that we, as culturally informed music therapists, are also human beings who can make a mistake. (Kenny, 2006; Scheiby, 2001).

It is human to admit that we are not flawless. Learning about cultures is a life-long task that is on a continuum of learning about human beings and their lives.

Clinical uses

The CIMT approach described in this chapter is particularly useful with immigrants because it considers the problems and issues that may arise during the acculturation process. If the approach is used for ethnic groups, specific cultural considerations must be made. Since this method has been developed with an emphasis on issues, gender-specific needs have to be addressed. Likewise, when the method is used on a population of children, appropriate modifications are necessary, according to their age and developmental stages. For people who have disabilities, this method can be used only with proper adaptations.

CIMT goals

The following primary goals are addressed in CIMT, in addition to the specific personal issues of the client:

- supporting the client's acculturation process
- identifying the cause of psychosomatic symptoms and working through the healing process by the use of music
- managing acculturative stress
- resolving acculturation conflicts
- facilitating the formulation of strategies and coping skills
- balancing the three layers of one's cultural being
- working toward a healthier level of cultural identity
- collaborating to change one's lifestyle so that it is more satisfactory within the context of family and the community
- establishing and practicing life strategies and resources
- integrating one's cognitive, psychological, and spiritual dimensions.

Session format

The session format is a combination of individual and group sessions. On completion of the assessment, the client will be recommended for individual, group, or dual sessions. The client recommended for individual sessions will eventually be transferred to group sessions:

> If we always deal with the difficulties of life in isolation, as the individual, and never relate ourselves to the whole, any solution or cure is likely to be merely an illusion, and short-lived. Many of the modern systems of therapy concentrate entirely on the individual. (Kenny, 2006, p.23)

Therefore, the last stage of CIMT is group work, which every client will have an opportunity to experience. It is noteworthy that people of non-Western backgrounds can be more private than others and maybe this is generally common in most non-Western cultures. In addition, confidentiality is very important for them, so more in-depth work may be done in individual sessions.

The group size is limited to a maximum of six to eight people, including the therapist who maximizes the benefit of the group and increases opportunities for clients to interact with one another. If available, male and female therapists can lead the session together. Since this is similar to having a father and mother figure in therapy, transferential reactions may arise more frequently. Also, a translator or family members may attend the sessions, if that is conducive to the therapeutic process.

The worldviews of music therapists and their clients actively negotiate as intersubjective cultural identities. Eventually, they create a transcending form of music community. Thus, every session should bridge this cultural gap.

Music experiences

In Korean culture, for example, "heart-to-heart communication" denotes non-verbal communication (Kim, 2007). Koreans are used to reading gestures, facial expressions, body posture, and other non-verbal cues. Because of culturally fostered difficulty in expressing feelings verbally, Koreans rely more on music for emotional expression

(Kim, 2007, 2013c). It can be a therapeutic experience when one uses music to express oneself, especially negative feelings, because it is non-threatening. In CIMT, both receptive and active music experiences are provided. In choosing to use either receptive or active experience, it is important for the therapist to consider the client's individual preferences. The same client might even need other modalities, depending on the day, the circumstance, and their communities.

Receptive music experience

Musical analytical meditation, a new AMT technique created by Scheiby (2013), can be used to address acculturation issues and explore the unconscious mind. As Scheiby shared (personal communication, 2013):

> During the musical meditation process, the client often enters a stage of consciousness that is similar to a dream state, and the symbols received from the subconscious can be experienced as dream-like. Just as symbolic material from dreams is worked within AMT to discover the solutions they offer for psychological issues, the images and symbols that come up during musical meditation are similarly analyzed.

There are five stages of musical analytical meditation: assessment, deepening the breath, musically accompanied traveling, verbal processing, and musical closure ritual. Depending on the client's needs and his or her functional level, this meditation can be performed by the client playing alone, together with the therapist, or by the therapist playing alone.

Active music experience

In CIMT, I incorporated AMT techniques by allowing the client to use all types of instruments and musical idioms, as improvisational music is used as symbolic expression (Priestley, 1994; Scheiby, 2015). It is also used to stimulate thoughts and feelings associated with one's life events. This enables clients, regardless of their cultural or musical backgrounds, to explore their individual issues. The client can play music, sing, talk, or do all three; they can also sit in silence. The clients' self-exploration is enhanced by this great freedom and a variety of mediums to express themselves better.

It is important to consider individual preference in whether receptive or active music experience is used. The same client might even need other modalities, depending on the day, the circumstance, and changes in his or her cultural being.

A wide variety of music in CIMT

Many people believe that cross-cultural factors between a therapist and a client can cause problems. In fact, traditional thinking in this area has only viewed the realm of cross-cultural factors in a problematic light. However, my belief is that such cross-cultural elements can actually be an advantage in therapy when there is a willingness to grow on the part of the client and the therapist. For example, a culturally informed therapist can use diverse cultural music to help a client prepare for living in a divergent society. This cultural understanding can help develop the client's life in a richer way. Therefore, we can use "differences" in a positive way, as Aigen (2002) stated:

> Different styles of music lend themselves to particular types of expression and experiences, and the music therapist who can bring forth different styles in the improvisational setting is better equipped to create the variety of moods and experiences individually suited for particular clients and circumstances. (p.9)

Some examples of music experience methods are described in "Stress reduction and wellness" (Kim, 2013c).

Assessment

Culturally informed music therapists must understand well influential factors such as acculturation, class, education, ethnic identity, within-group and between-group differences, religion and spirituality, and socio-political environmental factors including, racism, discrimination, prejudice, economic status, level of acculturation, and generational differences (American Music Therapy Association, 2019a, 2019b).

Cultural factors are very powerful influences in the development and the ongoing life of every individual, but they are not absolute determinants:

> The noted French sociologist Emile Durkheim stressed that culture is something outside us exerting a strong coercive power on us. We do not always feel the constraints of our culture because we generally conform to the types of conduct and thought it requires. Yet when we do try to oppose cultural constraints, their strength becomes apparent. (Swartz & Jordan, 1980, p.165)

This process of self-discovery and self-understanding has been a critically important part of my development as a music therapist and as an individual.

I find it effective to integrate three tools for the CIMT assessment: Scheiby's assessment (2001) Bruscia's Improvisation Assessment Profile (1987) and the multicultural assessment (Hadley & Norris, 2016; Pedersen et al., 2016). There are three major areas in assessment: musical, non-musical, and cultural.

The following are musical parameters: rhythm, melody, harmony, tempo, phrasing, themes or motifs, dynamics, choice and use of instruments/vocal, musical idioms, range, articulation, and timbre. Second, the following informational categories are identified in the music and described (Scheiby, 2001): affective, relational, cognitive, developmental, transpersonal, aesthetic, kinesthetic, creativity, energetic, listening skills, and cultural information. In addition, the worldview, cultural identity stage, and the acculturation of the client are included in the assessment:

- How is gender conceptualized?

- What is the socio-political history of the group to which the client belongs?

- What is the client's generational status?

- What is the status of the client's religious and/or spiritual belief?

- What is the client's stage of life?

- What languages does the client speak?

- Was migration of the client's group a free choice, or was it forced?

- How long have they lived in the US?

- What is the client's sexual orientation?

- What is the client's ability/disability status? What are their musical culture and family traditions?

Evaluation

Quarterly, semi-annual, and annual evaluations will take place. All the items described above will be evaluated. Family and community leaders can be a part of the evaluation team.

Therapy procedure

In typical AMT sessions, an issue is identified and a title is then suggested, usually by the therapist, on which to improvise. The selection of the AMT technique depends on the issue being explored. Sometimes, the client and therapist improvise without a title or focus. Feelings and reactions arising during the improvisation are usually verbally processed following the improvisation. Art, clay sculpture, imagery, movement, and body work are also ways in which to process these feelings and reactions (Priestley, 1975).

In CIMT, depending on the client's developmental stage and needs, this traditional procedure can be used or modified: 1) identifying an issue; 2) selecting a musical program: meditation, voicework, and so on; 3) sharing a musical experience; and 4) discussion.

Techniques

One size does not fit all. Culturally diverse clients often identify with more than one cultural group. This is why applying multiple modalities may be effective in sessions. Many indigenous cultures value multiple modality. Commonly, music and movement are inseparable, just as music and spirituality are inseparable. Utilizing multiple creative arts methods in a study is recommended.

Meditation

Through meditation, the client can bring mental processes under greater voluntary control. This will result in bringing out new levels of awareness, concentration, joy, love, and compassion: "developing the ability of the mind to focus attention without distraction on specific objects, such as the breath, an emotion, or sound. Awareness meditations, on the other hand, aim at exploring any experiences that occur" (Walsh, 1995, p.388). The aim is to develop optimal states of psychological well-being and consciousness. Meditation enhances longevity, confidence, self-esteem, empathy, and creativity. Healthy qualities such as mindfulness, love, compassion, concentration, and calmness can be cultivated.

Voicework

When working with women who have lost their voice due to socio-political reasons, I find it effective to do voicework accompanied by movement. As Uhlig (2006) noted, "Where does the voice come from? Everybody is born with a voice as a natural, biological instrument, which is becoming a cultural phenomenon through its adaptations" (p.45). The aim is to find their real voice so that the voice transforms from unheard to audible. Meditation, which helps the client concentrate, focus, and relax, is followed by work on voice and movement. Like entrainment and toning, using vowel sounds and listening to the emotional qualities of the voice are important factors in this work. In addition, making movements helps them to lessen their cultural stress levels. Depending on their developmental stages, the movements can be done by the clients themselves or with a therapist.

Psychodynamic Movement

The pyschodynamic movement was developed by Priestley and modified by Pedersen and Scheiby (Pedersen, 2002). It is a technique that is useful for clients from diverse cultures to gain greater insight into their own body, mind, and spirit. The tenets of this movement are as follows: "The core of psychodynamic movement is improvised movement by one or more persons on an agreed topic, accompanied by one or more persons who follow and interpret the movements in a parallel instrumental/voice improvisation." This is also called "improvised movement to improvised music" (Pedersen, 2002, p.191). This movement helps clients maintain their emotional well-being and develop strategies to deal with existing acculturative stress (some useful information is described in Chapter 5).

Stages of CIMT

The length of treatment varies according to individual needs. The therapy can be terminated when an individual has reached an integrated cultural self and is able to adjust adequately to the environment. It is highly recommended that ongoing support and culture-related stress reduction are essential for the immigrant population. Once the client develops unique coping skills for the meditation practice, it can be done in a peer group. Since this method emphasizes the importance of being in contact with people and the community as much as possible, practicing meditation alone is discouraged.

The role of music

Music as ritual

The client's status of cultural being is explored in a "ritual space": "Music is always a doorway to ritual space though not every person is able to go through it or recognize the place to which it leads. When we awaken to that recollection, the music takes us through in an instant" (Kenny, 2006, p.77). "Ritual" activities originated from ancient systems and are "a more intimate" earth connection. These activities reinforce the idea that we are part of the whole system and interrelated with one another. The wholeness represents both preventative and curative balances:

> Improving quality of life means that as persons we feel better about ourselves, less isolated in society, we keep the right balance between our roots (past tradition) and our present life, between our uniqueness and the group's identity. When we gather together, share and make music with each other, we feel less isolated. (Amir, 2004, p.254)

Music as cultural identity building

I believe that among all human experiences, music most closely expresses and elicits the cultural self of human beings. The aim of doing improvisation is to reflect unconscious dynamics so that this material can surface and ultimately reflect psychological, physical, spiritual, and cultural aspects of the client's intrapersonal and interpersonal lives. Therefore, music is an indicator of the client's status of cultural being (Halick, 2017; Higgins & Mantie, 2013). In turn, because music is an expression of culture, through musical experiences, it is possible that the client will develop a higher level of cultural awareness: "music mobilized in particular ways...is a key way of building cultural bridges, or helping re-socialization, acculturation and integrating into new cultural homes" (Pavlicevic & Ansdell, 2004, p.25).

Music as community building

Music provides a social space where we explore ourselves relating to ourselves and to others, while at times transcending time and space. Within the realm of the social space, there are opportunities for clients such that "new contacts may be established and other persons give us access to values and social experiences. Music becomes a social resource, a way of getting to know groups, communities and cultures" (Ruud, 1997, p.95).

Music as a transcending energy

Music helps transcend one's own culture and creates a new culture in the music therapy context—no boundary, no judgment, just clients connecting as human beings. When clients play music together in a group, they are able to bond with one another at a deep level. When their cultural entities actively engage in music and open to one another, the "click moment" of musical experience can take place. It might be because the magical aspect of music facilitates the almost-instant formation of alliance between them, because their individual connection to music already exists. It carries with it the feeling of being related, as though they are somehow members of a musical family.

We all share the secret that most clients who are not directly involved in music therapy groups do not know—the enchantment, the transforming power, the inherent transcendence of music, for all humans. Music helps us transcend time and space. It helps beyond our cultural boundaries and unites us as a collective culture.

Music as a cultural learning facilitator

Learning language is more than just learning vocabulary and grammar. It also involves the culture of the language, including feelings, history, and usage. Clients can gain benefits when learning English from songs or other musical activities. These benefits might be new vocabulary, idioms, and even customs, because music embodies so much of our culture (Blaking, 1995; Kim *et al.*, 2012).

Music as an acculturation stress reliever

When engaged in verbal interchanges, immigrant clients may seem to concentrate intently, in order to be certain that they understand what is being said and to correctly formulate their own thoughts in words. Although I believe that all people go through this to some degree, it is more demanding for them because English is their second language. However, when they are engaged in musical communication or self-expression, they are able to simply hear, feel, and intuitively understand the meaning of the music. This musical experience can provide a better sense of freedom and autonomy when compared to verbal discussion. In addition, because of their culturally fostered difficulty in expressing feelings verbally, they can rely on music as a means of expression. The clients feel relieved when they make an improvisation without words in English.

The role of a culturally informed music therapist

Cultural vessel

As a cultural vessel, culturally informed music therapists should have a good understanding of their own musical background and cultural endowment as well as the client's (Shapiro, 2005). Culturally informed music therapists work not only with their clients but also with their families and communities. The therapists' tasks entail increasing their own awareness of the client's culture and collaborating with the client to come up with possible solutions within their own cultural contexts. Therefore, the role of the therapist is to facilitate family relationships, empower clients to utilize their own resources, and activate community support systems.

Flexibility and openness to new environments

Culturally informed music therapists' flexibility in their attitudes and understanding of their clients' experiences are very important to build effective therapeutic relationships. In addition, the openness to their client, regardless of cultural match, is crucial. McFadden (1999) is also supportive of this position: "To understand cultural conditioning, one needs to move beyond the concept of race and ethnicity to understanding aspects that clarify the human condition in general and the specific way people consider their universe, the world, and the people and objects within it" (p.28).

Cultural empathy

Culturally informed music therapists know how important it is to express empathy to clients because humans are all cultural beings. Empathy has a large impact on the therapeutic relationship and the therapist's overall efficacy in addressing the client (Brown, 2002; Kim, 2008; Swamy & Kim, 2019).

Examples of CIMT applications
Crafting a cultural bridge in music therapy
Seung-A Kim, a culturally informed music therapist

When I started to practice music therapy many years ago, most of my clients were Americans. As a Korean-American music therapist, I witnessed how music therapy can help people in life, and I was eager to introduce music therapy to the Korean community. At first, I faced some challenges within the community. The cultural crashes between Korean and American norms were apparent. Parents often wanted me to teach their children to play the piano. There is a common Korean saying, "*PPali PPali.*" They wanted to see results right away. They thought music therapy was a miracle to cure all, but there was also a stigma. Some clients and parents refused music therapy and did not share the information pertinent to helping their child.

Since 2000, I have made efforts to introduce and promote music therapy to the Korean immigrant community in the Tri-State area. There are several projects I have undertaken for the community, and I would like to share them with you in this chapter. I hope this will be helpful in your current and future endeavors.

I created a music therapy program for Korean immigrant families in Bethpage, New York, to serve children, adolescents, and their families. The clients are bilingual and have learning disabilities, autism spectrum disorder (ASD); Korean-American Alliance for Creative Arts Therapy (KAACAT), and problems related to cultural adjustments. Another effort was made to organize Korean-licensed creative arts therapy meetings and provide workshops to members of the Korean community regularly. Most recently, I have been working closely with the Esther Ha Foundation, educating and promoting music therapy to Korean immigrant families. The three major projects this foundation has offered to the Korean community are a healing concert, a healing camp, and mental health education on a radio station.

As a music therapist, I have consulted with other health professionals to organize these healing concert events. The concert took place in October 2018, and we highlighted music therapy in the program, which consisted of receptive, compositional, and improvisational music therapy methods. There were a couple of well-known guest artists who performed songs matching the concert theme. Then we had a few clients who performed songs they wrote with music therapists in the sessions. Interaction with audiences was possible during community singing and the drum circle. Then, the "aha" moment! Over the years, I have witnessed the tears and openness Korean clients have demonstrated, as well as their appreciation. It might take time to build a relationship with Koreans, but once they build trust with you, they will be very open to you and pour out their emotions and expressions in music. We just need to think outside the box and utilize a variety of approaches to work with them.

Language considerations in conducting music therapy with children and young adults of Korean descent

Jon Reichert, MS, LCAT, MT-BC at SUNY Stony Brook Medicine

As a graduate music therapy student at Molloy College, I had the opportunity to do clinical fieldwork with one of my professors, Dr. Seung-A Kim. The site was a large Korean church, which offered various programs for Korean children, adolescents, and young adults with developmental delays, learning disabilities, and emotional issues. Dr. Kim led the music therapy program at the church.

I am a middle-aged, Caucasian male. While being excited at the prospect of doing clinical work with Dr. Kim, I was also somewhat apprehensive about working with this specific population, primarily because I do not speak Korean. When I initially voiced this concern to Dr. Kim, she assured me that language should not be a problem because most of the clients attended American schools, and their parents encouraged them to speak English in the church's programs as a way to further reinforce their use of English.

I was also concerned about the music to be used in the sessions. Would the music be mostly or entirely Korean songs? Would I need to spend time learning an entirely new, culturally specific list of songs which would then have limited applicability when working with other populations? In general, I was apprehensive about working with a population that I perceived could be culturally quite different from my own.

Overall, I found the clients to very accepting of me and generally willing to participate in the suggested musical interventions. When I first met most of them, there were no apparent distinctions between their own cultural background and my own. A few clients seemed particularly intrigued by me and my presence in the sessions.

When I first arrived at the site, I discovered that it was a very large facility, with a congregation of about 1500. The clients had various levels of developmental delays and learning disabilities, were at various points on the autism spectrum, and one had cerebral palsy. Dr. Kim said they were "1.5 generation Americans," meaning they were born in Korea but moved to the US before becoming young adults. The clients who were verbal were all fluent in English, although Korean was likely the primary language spoken in their homes. There were some clients that Dr. Kim and I worked with for only a short duration, but during my time at the church there were three individuals and a small group of two to three members that we worked with on a consistent basis.

The songs used in the sessions were primarily sung in English, with an occasional Korean song. When working with these clients, we felt it was important to acknowledge their cultural heritage, and one way of doing that was to incorporate Korean words and culture into our musical interventions. One simple practice was to use the Korean word for "hello," which is "anyoung," in our greeting songs. I learned that different cultures have different human vocalizations for the sounds that animals make. So, when singing "Old MacDonald," rather than singing "cluck-cluck" for a chicken, a Korean chicken would make more of a "cuuk-cuuk" sound.

One individual client we worked with was Seon, a male in his late teens. He had moved to the US from Korea within the last 18 months. Seon was one of the higher functioning clients. He presented as very affable during our sessions but had anger management issues as well as depression.

Seon preferred to have his sessions conducted in Korean because he was not fluent in English. He seemed to appreciate my presence in his sessions because, as he was developing his English-speaking skills, he liked to try them out on me. He was somewhat tentative, preferring to ask his questions of me in Korean to Dr. Kim, and then have her translate them into English for me. However, when Dr. Kim prompted him to ask me directly in English, he usually did. Seon was knowledgeable about contemporary Korean pop music stars, and he introduced me to K-pop.

After we'd been working together for a couple of months, Seon asked if we could listen to a recording of the Korean song "1000 Winds," which was about the disastrous ferry accident that had happened in Korea earlier that year, where several hundred people drowned, many of them high school students. This song became the main focus of his sessions going forward. Initially, we would just listen to the song during the session. Dr. Kim asked Seon if he knew anyone directly impacted by the ferry accident, and he replied that he did not. She asked him how the song made him feel, and all he said was, "sad." From the somber look on his face as we listened to the song, it appeared to be having an emotional impact on him. In subsequent sessions, Seon began singing along to the recording, and Dr. Kim and I eventually began accompanying him on piano and guitar. Seon told us that he wanted to perform the song for the church's congregation sometime.

Why was Seon so taken with this song? As a recent immigrant to the US, Seon had experienced his own losses: his culture, friends, familiar surroundings, as well as his ability to easily communicate. It appeared that Seon was using "1000 Winds" to help him process his grief from his own loss, and as a means of communicating his grief.

Conclusion

What we see is what we perceive, which leads to what we believe. What I have come to believe is that there is not just one rigid method that is effective for all clients. As Pavlicevic and Ansdell (2004) stated, "In the twenty-first century, wherever we practice, we can no longer simply state that music therapy is 'such and such' a practice, described with the help of 'such and such' theories, without addressing a crucial third bit: context" (p.45). In the past, differences between cultures were considered negative. To work with culturally diverse clients, thinking outside the box is helpful. Rather than waiting for clients to come, music therapists must go to them, work closely with community leaders and other professionals, and continue to educate about the benefits of music therapy. I see difference as a strength, wholeness, and an opportunity to expand one's horizons. The differences among people can stimulate the expansion of one's worldview. Expanding the self can be achieved by fluidity on the part of the therapist, and sharing that fluidity with the client and the community. As Bruscia (2000) stated, "We have to celebrate differences. We have to move in and out of them" (p.95). Such a cross-cultural experience can actually be advantageous in life, such that when one faces a new environment, it is possible to understand that "variety is the spice of life." As I worked with the clients over time and the therapeutic relationship developed and strengthened, any differences in our cultural backgrounds seemed to become less obvious and less relevant. I evolved from thinking of them as Korean clients to approaching them as clients who were of Korean descent, and incorporating that culture into the musical experiences. Working with these clients was a very unique and rewarding experience. Thus, the culturally informed music therapists' methods are constantly moving, connecting, and reconnecting to the past, present, and future, as their cultural beings have expanded to the ultimate state of health.

References

Abrams, B. (2015). "Music Therapy and Cultural Diversity." In B. L. Wheeler (ed.), *Music Therapy Handbook*. New York, NY: Guilford Press.

Adler, A. (1959). *Understanding Human Nature*. New York, NY: Premier Books.

Aigen, K. (1997). "Here we are in music: One year with an adolescent. Creative Music Therapy group." *Nordorff-Robbins Music Therapy Monograph Series #2*. St. Louis, MO: MMB Music.

Aigen, K. (2002). *Playin' in the band: A qualitative study of popular music styles as clinical improvisation*. Nordoff-Robbins Center for Music Therapy, Steinhardt School of Education: New York University.

American Music Therapy Association (2019a). *Professional Competencies*. Retrieved from www.musictherapy.org/about/competencies.

American Music Therapy Association (2019b). *Code of Ethics*. Retrieved from www.musictherapy.org/about/ethics.

Amir, D. (2004). "Community Music Therapy and the Challenge of Multiculturalism." In M. Pavlicevic & G. Ansdell (eds), *Community Music Therapy*. London and Philadelphia: Jessica Kingsley Publishers.

Beer, L. E. (2015). "Crisscrossing cultural divides: Experiences of U.S. trained Asian music therapists." *Qualitative Inquiries in Music Therapy: A Monograph Series,* 10(1), 127–173.

Berry, J. W. (1997). "Immigration, acculturation, and adaptation." *Applied Psychology,* 46(1), 5–34.

Berry, J. W., Kim, U., Minde, T., & Mok, D. (1987). "Comparative studies of acculturative stress." *International Migration Review,* 21(3), 491–511.

Blacking, J. (1995). *Music, Culture & Experience.* Chicago, IL: The University of Chicago Press.

Brown, J. M. (2002). "Towards a Culturally Centered Music Therapy Practice." In C. Kenny & B. Stige (eds), *Contemporary Voices in Music Therapy: Communication, Culture, and Community* (pp. 83–94). Olso, Norway: Unipub Forlag.

Bruscia, K. (1987). *Improvisational Models of Music Therapy.* Gilsum, NH: Barcelona Publishers.

Bruscia, K. (2000). "The nature of meaning in music therapy." *Nordic Journal of Music Therapy,* 9(2), 84–96.

Bruscia, K. E. (ed.). (2012). *Self-Experiences in Music Therapy Education, Training, and Supervision.* Gilsum, NH: Barcelona Publishers.

Bruscia, K. (2014). *Defining Music Therapy.* Gilsum, NH: Barcelona Publishers.

Epstein, M. (1998). *Going to Pieces Without Falling Apart.* New York, NY: Broadway Books.

Hadley, S. & Norris, M. (2016). "Musical multicultural competency in music therapy: The first step." *Music Therapy Perspectives,* 34(2), 129–137.

Halick, M. E. (2017). "Neuroscience, music, and culture: Finding pathways to effective multicultural music education." *Update: Applications of Research in Music Education,* 35(3), 11–15.

Hall, E. T. (1982). *The Therapeutic Value of Music.* Los Angeles, CA: The Philosophical Research Society.

Higgins, L. & Mantie, R. (2013). "Improvisation as ability, culture, and experience." *Music Educators Journal,* 100(2), 38–44. Retrieved from www.jstor.org/stable/43288813.

Kenny, C. (2006). *Music & Life in the Field of Play: An Anthology.* Gilsum, NH: Barcelona Publishers.

Kenny, C. & Stige, B. (2002). *Contemporary Voices in Music Therapy: Communication, Culture, and Community.* Oslo, Norway: Oslo Academic Press.

Kim, E. H. (1995). "Home is Where the Han Is." In K. Mehuron & G. Percesepe (eds) *Free Spirits: Feminist Philosophers on Culture* (pp.160–173). Englewood Cliffs, NJ: Prentice Hall.

Kim, S. (2007). "Feminism and Music Therapy in Korea." In S. Hadley (ed.), *Feminist Perspectives on Music Therapy* (pp.127–156). Gilsum, NH: Barcelona Publishers.

Kim, S. (2008). "The supervisee's experience in cross-cultural music therapy supervision." *Qualitative Inquiries in Music Therapy: A Monograph Series,* 4, 1–44.

Kim, S. (2011). "Predictors of acculturative stress among international music therapy students in the U.S." *Music Therapy Perspectives*, 29(2), 126–132.

Kim, S. (2013a, April). *Multicultural Training for the Healthcare Professionals and Students*. Poster presentation at the Conference of the Mid-Atlantic Region of AMTA, Scranton, PA.

Kim, S. (2013b). "Re-discovering voice: Korean immigrant women in group music therapy." *Arts in Psychotherapy*, 40(4), 428–435.

Kim, S. (2013c). "Stress Reduction and Wellness." In L. Eyre (ed.), *Guidelines for Music Therapy Practice in Mental Health: A Four-Volume Series* (pp.797–839). Gilsum, NH: Barcelona Publishers.

Kim, S. & Elefant, C. (2016). "Multicultural Considerations in Music Therapy Research." In B. L. Wheeler (ed.), *Music Therapy Research* (third edition). Gilsum, NH: Barcelona Publishers.

Kim, S., Sairam, T., Shapiro, N., & Swamy, S. (2012, March). *When a Paradigm Shifts: Therapeutic Applications of Music Therapy across Cultures*. Presentation at the Conference of the Mid-Atlantic Region of AMTA, Baltimore, MD.

Kim, S. & Whitehead-Pleaux, A. (2015). "Music Therapy and Cultural Diversity." In B. L. Wheeler (ed.), *Music Therapy Handbook*. New York, NY: Guilford Press.

Lee, J. H. (2015). "Integral thinking in music therapy." *Journal of Music and Human Behavior*, 12(1), 65–94.

McFadden, J. (ed.) (1999). *Transcultural Counseling* (second edition). Alexandria: VA, American Counseling Association.

Pavlicevic, M. & Ansdell, G. (2004). *Community Music Therapy*. London and Philadelphia: Jessica Kingsley Publishers.

Pedersen, P. B., Draguns, J. G., Lonner, W. J., & Trimble, J. E. (eds) (2016). *Counseling Across Cultures* (seventh edition). Thousand Oaks, CA: Sage Publications.

Piaget, J. (1976). *The Grasp of Consciousness: Action and Concept in the Young Child*. (S. Wedgewood, Trans.). Cambridge, MA: Harvard University Press,

Priestley, M. (1975). *Music Therapy in Action*. St. Louis, MO: Magnamusic-Baton.

Priestley, M. (1994). *Essays on Analytical Music Therapy*. Phoenixville, PA: Barcelona Publishers.

Roland, A. (1996). *Cultural Pluralism and Psychoanalysis: The Asian and North American Experience*. New York, NY and London, UK: Routledge.

Ruud, E. (1997). *Music Therapy: Improvisation, Communication, and Culture*. Gilsum, NH: Barcelona Publishers.

Saarikallio, S. (2012). "Cross-Cultural Approaches to Music and Health." In R. R. Macdonald, G. Kreutz, & L. Mitchell (eds), *Music, Health, and Wellbeing* (pp.477–490). Oxford, UK: Oxford University Press.

Scheiby, B. B. (2001). "Forming an Identity as a Music Psychotherapist through Analytical Music Therapy Supervision." In M. Forinash (ed.) *Music Therapy Supervision*. Gilsum, NH: Barcelona Publishers.

Scheiby, B. B. (2013). "Analytical Music Therapy for Pain Management and Reinforcement of Self-Directed Neuroplasticity in Patients Recovering from Medical Trauma." In J. Mondanaro & G. Sara (eds), *Music and Medicine: Integrative Models in Pain Medicine* (pp.149–179). New York, NY: Satchnote Press.

Scheiby, B. B. (2015). "Analytical Music Therapy." In B. L. Wheeler (ed.), *Music Therapy Handbook* (pp.206–219). New York, NY: Guilford Press.

Shapiro, N. (2005). "Sounds in the world: Multicultural influences in music therapy in clinical practice and training." *Music Therapy Perspectives*, 23(1), 29–35.

Spector, R. E. (2012). *Cultural Diversity in Health and Illness* (sixth edition). Upper Saddle River, NJ: Prentice Hall.

Stige, B. (2002). *Culture-Centered Music Therapy*. Gilsum, NH: Barcelona Publishers.

Stige, B. & Aarø, L. E. (2012). *Invitation to Community Music Therapy*. New York, NY: Routledge.

Stige, B., Ansdell, G., Elefant, C., & Pavlicevic, M. (2010). *Where Music Helps: Community Music Therapy in Action and Reflection*. Farnham, UK: Ashgate.

Sue, D. W. & Sue. D. (2013). *Counseling the Culturally Different: Theory and Practice* (seventh edition). New York, NY: John Wiley & Sons.

Swamy, S. (2014). "Music therapy in the global age: Three keys to successful culturally centered practice." *The New Zealand Journal of Music Therapy*, 12, 34–57.

Swamy, S. & Kim, S. (2019). "Culturally Responsive Academic Supervision." In M. Forinash (ed.), *Music Therapy Supervision* (second edition). Gilsum, NH: Barcelona Publishers.

Swartz, M. J. & Jordan, D. K. (1980). *Culture: The Anthropological Perspectives*. San Diego, CA: John Wiley & Sons.

Uhlig, S. (2006). *Authentic Voices, Authentic Singing: A Multicultural Approach to Vocal Music Therapy*. Gilsum, NH: Barcelona Publishers.

Vandervoort, A. E. (2017). Culturally relevant music therapy in the southwestern United States: An investigation of music therapy with Hispanic populations (Order No. 10592849). ProQuest Dissertations & Theses Global. (1896118112). Retrieved from https://shsu-ir.tdl.org/handle/20.500.11875/2194

Vera, E. M. & Speight, S. L. (2003). "Multicultural competence, social justice, and counseling psychology: Expanding our roles." *The Counseling Psychologist*, 31(3), 253–272. doi:10.1177/0011000003031003001.

Walsh, R. (1995). "Asian Psychotherapies." In R. J. Corsini & D. Wedding (eds). *Current Psychotherapies* (fifth edition). Itasca, IL: F. E. Peacock Publications.

Whitehead-Pleaux, A. & Tan, X. (2017). *Cultural Intersections: Music, Health, and the Person*. Gilsum, NH: Barcelona Publishers.

Wilber, K. (1979). *No Boundary*. Boston, MA: Shambhala.

Yalom, I. D. (1995). *The Theory and Practice of Group Psychotherapy* (fourth edition). New York, NY: Basic Books.

Musical and Cultural Considerations for Building Rapport in Music Therapy Practice

Kamica King, MA, MT-BC

A first-generation Trinidadian-American, I grew up in an intercultural environment among many other immigrant families. With music as a central staple in my family's household, you could hear R&B/ soul, gospel, soca, reggae, hip-hop, rock, jazz, pop, and even a dash of country playing at any given time. Family friends hailed from five of the seven continents, so in addition to the fusion of Trinidadian and American culture that influenced my upbringing, I was exposed to a host of cultural customs, foods, and music from all over the world. I attended a pre-kindergarten program intentionally housed in a healthcare center for older adults that provided meaningful opportunities for intergeneration interaction from a young age as well.

All of these experiences provided a foundation that helped me to begin to learn about others. In my approach, I foremost honor the humanity in others, connecting at the points of similarity, while also seeking to understand the differences. What I didn't know at that time was that those intercultural and musical experiences of my youth would help prepare me to naturally build rapport with clients who, from session to session or even within the same session, come from diverse cultural backgrounds and generations, with varied life experiences and musical preferences.

While the experiences of my upbringing may resonate with some who are reading this, over time I came to realize that experiences of deep connection with diverse groups of people were not as common as I had thought among colleagues or the students I supervised. Some came from very homogeneous communities, whether that community's lack of diversity was by default or design. With regard to practicum supervision, a few common challenges surfaced among students training in diverse psychiatric, medical, and community settings focused on adult mental health and psychosocial goal areas. These were: limited knowledge of contemporary music history, a lack of familiarity with music outside a narrow scope of genres, and uncertainty about how to engage with a client they perceived as having significantly more and/or different life experiences than them.

Another trend was that as students were still learning how to practice music therapy, a strong focus on what to do next would often take them away from being present with the client in the moment. That would equal missed cues from the client in real time that could have positively informed the student's clinical decision-making process. Some students were so used to the ability to fully carry out a session plan as written that when a situation required on-the-spot adaptation, they would have great difficulty. Working in settings where the age can range from 18 to 95 with seemingly as many cultural backgrounds, I found that the ability to build authentic rapport, exercise cultural humility, and adapt to the needs of the client(s) in real time was imperative to success in these environments.

Therefore, the challenges the students faced required additional supervision that spoke to their development both intrapersonally and interpersonally, while laying the foundation for them to learn, grow and exercise cultural humility. This chapter shares many of those elements, with a focus on building rapport, cultural considerations in music therapy practice, and thoughtfully expanding one's musical repertoire and knowledgebase to meet clients' needs.

In my work as a music therapist in Dallas, Texas, one of the ten largest metropolitan cities in the US, the clients and patients I see in both community-based and medical settings come from a variety of cultural backgrounds (U.S. Census Bureau, 2018). Though most often clients differ with regard to ethnicity, belief system, socio-economic status, age, and ability, the differences also show up in musical preferences and cultural - and generation-based thoughts on therapy.

In this chapter I will draw from my experience working with adult clients and their families, addressing mental health needs primarily in outpatient oncology, as well as inpatient psychiatric and community-based settings. The terms "patient" and "client" will be used interchangeably. Tools for practice will also be discussed.

Introduction

A review of the literature regarding music therapy and rapport showed that while the term "rapport" was often seen in the literature, it was not the direct focus of the material, and generally went undefined, alluding to it being considered a universally understood concept (Darrow & Johnson, 2009; Silverman, Letwin, & Neuhring, 2016; Williams & Abad, 2005). In addition, while much of the music therapy literature communicates that rapport is an essential element early in the therapeutic process, few sources explicitly detail the steps to be taken to establish and build authentic rapport with clients (Bolger, McFerran, & Stige, 2018; Rolvsjord, 2016; Silverman, 2019).

With so much of the process of building rapport being implied and/or hidden in studies and chapters that are more broadly focused, I've distilled the most applicable information from music therapy and counseling literature as well as my own experience as a practicing music therapist. This content is meant to provide a framework to include ways of thinking and being that can inform practice when it comes to not only establishing rapport, but doing so across cultures. While culture and ethnicity are often used synonymously, culture is a broad term that also encompasses beliefs, customs, communication styles, ideas, and values central to a group of people (Gallardo *et al.* 2012).

For every person, their unique mix of the aforementioned yields a blueprint for living and interpreting reality through their cultural lens based on what they've been taught by others and what they've learned through lived experience. Therefore, awareness of, knowledge about, and the demonstration of respect towards our clients and their culture are of great significance to the therapeutic process. While it's impossible to know everything about every culture we may encounter in our work as music therapists, it is imperative that we take our clients' culture(s) into account to inform our approach and practice, and to move towards an equitable experience for all the clients we serve (Chase, 2003; Dileo, 2000; Kim & Whitehead-Pleaux, 2015).

In synthesizing music therapy literature on building rapport, building trust and being genuine were themes that emerged (Baker, 2014; Grocke & Wigram, 2007; Hanser, 1999). Other aspects of the literature typified verbal, non-verbal, and musical techniques to engage clients early on, including asking open-ended questions, being mindful about body language, using preferred music, and engaging in improvisatory musical play (Baker, 2014; Bruscia, 1989; Jones, Baker & Day, 2004; Sadovnik, 2016; Silverman, 2019).

While rapport isn't explicitly mentioned in the book, *Music Therapy: A Fieldwork Primer*, Borzcon (2004) outlines a variety of personal and professional attributes that align with the elements needed to establish and build rapport, including having a genuine interest in people, exercising empathy, openness to new ideas, and being caring and professional (Leach, 2005). These attributes are based on the American Music Therapy Association's (AMTA) (n.d.) overview of the personal qualifications of a music therapist.

Culture: Competence, humility, and consciousness

Cultural competence "can be defined as the acquisition and maintenance of culture-specific skills required to (a) function effectively within a new cultural context and/or (b) interact effectively with people from different cultural backgrounds" (Wilson, Ward, & Fischer, 2013, p.900). The AMTA's Code of Ethics (2019) uses similar language, encouraging therapists to "acquire knowledge and information about the specific cultural group(s)." However, given the complexity of culture and the many layers that make up a singular identity, the term "cultural competence" has been critiqued, particularly with older definitions implying an achievable stopping point, rather than a lens through which one can be immersed in an inclusive, evolving way of being and thinking when it comes to learning about another's culture (Patallo, 2019; Tervalon & Murray-Garcia, 1998).

Rather than competence through acquisition, the idea of striving for cultural humility has gained traction over time as a more equitable and just term, strengthening the connection from theory into practice. Cultural humility is defined as "an others-oriented stance that seeks to develop mutual partnerships that address power imbalances with interpersonal respect, as well as a lifelong commitment to openness to new cultural information, critical self-examination of cultural awareness, and motivation to learn from others" (Upshaw, Lewis & Nelson, 2019, p.2).

Similarly, in the ways that we will likely encounter a wide variety of clients throughout our careers, we should aim to be culturally conscious in our efforts and deliver equitable, quality services to all. This concept of cultural consciousness is a process that entails increasing our awareness of culture, including that of our own and others' (Páez & Albert, 2012; Kumagai & Lypson, 2009). Knowledge of culture is one thing, but awareness, understanding, and the ongoing expansion of the aforementioned signify a deeper comprehension, similar to the difference in relationship between you and a close friend versus someone who is just an acquaintance. To take it a step further, once the aforementioned elements are in place, action in the form of putting what you have learned into practice is a necessary next step. While the Certification Board for Music Therapists (CBMT) may be alluding to cultural consciousness in their *Board Certification Domains*, in our field of music therapy, there is not enough of a basis for practice beyond the ideology and no formal cultural training in the curriculum that would hint at those discrepancies being addressed to evolve the future of the field (Certification Board for Music Therapists, 2015; Kim & Whitehead-Pleaux, 2015).

Rapport and the therapeutic process

Within the music therapy process, there are several elements that go into creating the proper "formula" for therapeutic work to take place. With variance in the theories and philosophies that anchor the ways in which music therapy is practiced, the formula, approach, and emphasis can be different depending on who you ask. At the same time, there does seem to be an element that is universal—the necessity to build rapport with clients in order to develop a beneficial working relationship; the client–therapist relationship, also known as the therapeutic relationship. As it relates to clinical foundations, the AMTA (2013) states that therapists should exercise "appropriate self-disclosure, authenticity, empathy, etc. toward affecting desired therapeutic outcomes." The aforementioned elements can be viewed as essential components of the building blocks of rapport. Designed to be a springboard for further exploration, this section will provide a brief overview of rapport and some of the key elements it is comprised of as it relates to the therapeutic process.

Rapport is the result of interactions where there is synergy and connection; "a conscious feeling of…trust, empathy, and mutual responsiveness between two or more people…that fosters the therapeutic process" (Farlex Partner Medical Dictionary, 2012). Rooted in communication, both verbal and non-verbal, building rapport requires "genuineness, openness, and warmth," as well as active listening and acceptance through a "non-judgmental posture" (Hanser, 1999, p.62). This posturing is not solely about physical positioning and body language, but also encompasses tone of voice, affect, and the overall presence of the music therapist.

Authenticity

From a basic humanities standpoint, at their core, clients want to be heard, understood, accepted, and cared for. Approaching clients from a place of authenticity, while communicating positive regard for them, is key in the establishment of the therapeutic relationship (Dileo, 2000; Silverman, 2019). Thinking about this as it pertains to working with adults addressing psychosocial goal areas, if a client is able to detect that you are genuine, approachable, and competent, trust can begin to be built if they are open to it. Your posturing, confidence and communication, both in style and content, go into the larger view of how your client perceives and, in turn, receives you.

As some of this information is abstract in that it describes a way of being rather than concrete actions, below is a sampling of directives from Borzcon (2004) to help guide the therapist, as detailed in *Music Therapy: A Fieldwork Primer*:

> Generally speaking, your affect needs to be one of acceptance. Your eyes need to be focused on the client in a way that allows the client to find safety within them. You need to observe, be present within the session, and not stare. You need to smile when appropriate and have it be natural and not contrived. Your body language should signal to the client that you are comfortable within the session and with him/her. (p.10)

Though Borzcon (2004) writes this specifically about affect, those directives can also be applied to approaching your client in a welcoming and authentic way.

Empathy

Expressing empathy toward a client communicates an inherent understanding of them that can deepen the therapeutic bond and create space for the client to open up more (Dileo, 2000). Empathy is "a complex capability enabling individuals to understand and feel the emotional states of others," something that Valentino (2006) stresses as more than just being present with a client (Riess, 2017, p.76). There is a sensing and a knowing on account of the therapist that has to take place in order for the experience to be categorized as empathy, an intrinsic download of information from the client about their world. Of note is that this informational download can be rooted in a cognitive process of deduction based on an automated cycle of assessment and evaluation, or it may stem from a more intuitive or instinct-based place, featuring an "inner knowing" that isn't able to be rationalized in the same way as the cognitive process (Brucsia, 1998; Brescia, 2005). Empathy is just one example of the interplay and nuances that go into building rapport and co-constructing an effective therapeutic relationship.

Food for thought: When in session with a client, what are some ways that you can communicate empathy?

Ideas: Is your demeanor warm and inviting? Do your responses and your body language communicate care and consideration, respect and understanding? Consider a time when someone demonstrated warmth and understanding. What characteristics made you feel their warmth and understanding?

Intersubjectivity

While with empathy the therapist expresses it towards the client, intersubjectivity takes it a step further in that it is a shared, interpersonal process. Intersubjectivity is a bi-directional, co-constructed exchange of "conscious information, knowledge, or emotions between individuals" where there is "joint attention" and a "shared world of meaning" as it relates to the therapeutic relationship (Trondalen, 2019, p.2; Reber, Allen, & Reber, 2009). In the *Penguin Dictionary of Psychology*, Reber, Allen, & Reber (2009) present a definition of intersubjectivity that conceptualizes the therapeutic relationship, denoting the verbal and non-verbal elements of the exchange and also presenting room to negotiate or even usurp hierarchical systems through an emphasis on mutuality and empathy. Within music therapy, intersubjectivity is also examined as it pertains to music-making and the musical relationship (Arthur, 2018; Birnbaum, 2014, Scheiby, 2005; Trondalen, 2019).

Self-awareness

Exercising self-awareness means getting to know yourself well and understanding what you bring to the session not only as a therapist, but foremost as a person. Who you are informs how you interact with clients. In the ways that building rapport is a cornerstone of the therapeutic relationship between client and therapist, the foundation of that relationship is a person-to-person connection; a human connection (Dileo, 2000; Rolvsjord, 2009). This intertwining of our personal and professional selves is solidified in Cormier, Nurius, and Osborn's (2009) writings on the professional skills of people in helping professions comprising: a) personal characteristics, b) training, c) academic knowledge, and d) clinical knowledge.

The practice of self-awareness allows you to take inventory of yourself, identifying your thoughts, attitudes, and how those display in your daily and clinical interactions. Self-awareness is also an important tool to recognize your own personal bias and examine its impact on the therapeutic process—an essential part of working with clients of different cultural backgrounds (Pieterse *et al.*, 2013).

The internal and personal work you do as a part of the process of being self-aware can also help you recognize countertransference, process feelings about transference, connect to your client, and vice versa. If you are wondering how to begin this exploration, consider seeking supervision or entering into therapy as a client (American Music Therapy Association, 2019; Chase, 2003; Hahna, 2017).

Active listening

In their chapter entitled "Cancer Care," McDougal-Miller and O'Callaghan (2010) explain that some clinicians, particularly those who are new, may miss information, context and cues for clients if they are too focused on planning next steps in session during opportunities to actively listen to the client. In contrast, remaining fully present when clients share leaves room for the information the therapist is receiving to guide next steps and intervention choices naturally, and at appropriate transitional times. To further examine the processes of active listening, let's take a look at how the *Encyclopedia of Child Behavior and Development* defines it: "Active listening entails the listener's involvement in hearing for intellectual and emotional messages. The listening focus is with what the person is saying, while confirming the accuracy of the content and the effect of the message" (Teniente & Guerra 2011, p.27). Of note is that the confirmation process happens through dialogue directly with the speaker to verify message meaning periodically. Deeper than verbatim, a client may ascribe meaning through implication rather than direct (explicit) verbalization, resulting in a duality between what is being said and the deeper levels of what is also being implied. Teniente and Guerra (2011) describe this process as "identifying explicit and implicit patterns of communication" where "verbal communications are received and reflected along with the underlying expression of feelings in an attempt to understand or explain a core message." Silverman (2019) also writes about active listening as a sign of respect for the client that contributes to the therapeutic alliance.

Verbal processing

As a practicum supervisor, particularly in mental health and medical settings, I find that students tend to have trouble figuring out how to respond to patients in real time during music therapy experiences that yield opportunities for verbal processing. Sometimes clients are facing situations and expressing difficult emotions that can be hard for students to process, let alone figure out the "right words to say" in response. In those instances, I remind them that the clients seek a safe space to be heard first and foremost, so their demeanor, affect, and posturing will set the tone beyond words. Clients want to be understood, so active listening, and being present in the moment with them goes a long way. I have also found that clients are not typically looking for advice, but rather the room to explore, express, and make sense of things for themselves. Validation, paraphrasing, and reflecting are techniques that can be used to provide support and encourage clients as they open up. Each technique is related to a verbal response from the therapist that provides a space for the client to confirm, clarify, and further process their thoughts (cognitive) and feelings (affective) (Cormier & Hackney, 2008). Validation involves understanding, accepting, and affirming the information the client shares (Kim & Kim, 2013; Oxford Living Dictionary, n.d.). When it comes to paraphrasing and reflecting, Cormier and Hackney (2008) differentiate between the two, sharing that paraphrasing focuses on rephrasing the cognitive, while reflecting involves responding to the affective content shared in session.

If students are still stuck trying to figure out appropriate responses, I implement a role-playing exercise to help them further develop their response mindset. During that exercise, I ask them to think about how they would respond if they were talking to a friend. The next part of the exercise is to explore that response and ways to filter it to be appropriate for use with a client. The trick is that the "friend" experience can feel more practical and relatable for the student, while filtering the response for the professional environment works toward preserving the integrity and ethics of the client–therapist relationship.

Self-disclosure

Self-disclosure "refers to the process of revealing personal…information about oneself to others" (Brunell, 2007, p.81). It is a therapeutic technique sometimes used by the therapist to build trust and foster a deeper connection with the client. At the same time, it is important to institute boundaries around the content and context in which the therapist shares personal information, so that the focus of music therapy remains on the client and their needs (Cormier & Hackney, 2008; Silverman, 2019). It is important to note that self-disclosure must be ethically sound and professionally warranted so that the differences between the therapeutic relationship and that of a friendship are clear, thus avoiding the presence of a dual relationship (Rolvsjord, 2009). This is critical toward the session remaining client-focused.

Discussion question: During an assessment (or introductory session), the patient turns to you after answering a few questions and says, "So tell me about yourself." How do you respond?

Food for thought:

- What might their reasons be for asking you that?

- Is the patient seeking to shift focus away from themself?

- Are they just curious and wanting to learn more about you or your qualifications?

Cultural considerations in music therapy practice

In the music therapy setting, the client is invited to communicate their thoughts, feelings, and needs to the extent in which they are comfortable. Within that, as a part of our clinical foundation as music therapists, we are to "demonstrate awareness of the influence of race, ethnicity, language, religion, marital status, gender, gender identity or expression, sexual orientation, age, ability, socioeconomic status, or political affiliation on the therapeutic process" (American Music Therapy Association, 2013). To take that concept a step further beyond awareness, cultural humility should be activated. Of note is that at times, the client's communication of their needs may be a) a non-verbal process, b) an indirect verbal process (implied), or c) an unconscious process. Thinking about styles of communication culturally, people communicate, emote, and choose what levels of information to disclose, based on the rules of their culture. These are often unwritten rules inherent to the identity and operations of that culture. The process of active listening can help the therapist decipher and accurately derive meaning from the content shared by the client.

Challenges of the colorblind approach

Due to the fact that there are so many nuances to cross-cultural interactions, for some, it may seem best to circumvent culture all together, only looking at the person's individual qualities and character, but not race, ethnicity, or any other aspects of culture (Williams, 2001). In the ways that our professional responsibilities call for us to "Conduct [ourselves] in an authentic, ethical, accountable, and culturally sensitive manner that respects privacy, dignity, and human rights," the colorblind approach goes directly against our duties to be both culturally sensitive and respectful when it comes to working with clients from all backgrounds (American Music Therapy Association, 2013; Certification Board for Music Therapists, 2020, p.4).

This colorblind lens also disregards culture in a way that strips a person of what may be an essential part of their identity. This is because it ignores cultural factors that affect how your patient views the world and how the world views your patient (Curtis, 2017; Hadley, 2017; Williams, 2001). Operating from a colorblind lens can bring a false sense of equality that may not apply to your patient's reality, particularly outside the session. It can also damage the strength of the therapeutic relationship in terms of equity, inclusion, personal agency, and power dynamics if the client is not recognized as a whole person, but rather as just the fragmented pieces the therapist prefers to acknowledge (Hahna, 2017; Kim & Whitehead-Pleaux, 2015; Rafieyan, 2017).

It can be difficult to know where to start when it comes to recognizing and dismantling stereotypes and biases, but starting with self-awareness of these constructs at play within the self can help you uncover and eventually dismantle those in existence personally and professionally. Seeking supervision from a qualified, culturally adept professional can aid your process as well (Chase, 2003; Hadley & Norris, 2016).

Assessment and treatment planning

The AMTA (2013) calls for therapists to "recognize the impact of one's own feelings, attitudes, and actions on the client and the therapy process." This recognition is important because, for example, during assessment, even unknowingly asking a client questions based on stereotypes can limit the scope of content, resulting in critical information being missed. Caution should be taken against stereotyping, where opinions about interactions and discoveries with one person (or group) are applied en masse to a belief that all people of that culture are the same way (Kim & Whitehead-Pleaux, 2015). Instead, the process should be multidimensional, as the CBMT board certification domain on assessment advises us to "identify a client's cultural...background in a number of ways" (2015, 2020, p.55). A thorough, culturally sensitive assessment is necessary to help provide a well-rounded understanding of the client, including how they view and express themselves and their culture. An individualized assessment process is imperative as when you meet someone from a particular culture, you're meeting a unique individual and should not default to working with them solely based on your past knowledge of that culture (Chase, 2003).

At the same time, when approached ethically and without bias or assumption, it can be of great benefit to mentally index facts about a culture like language, music, customs, and beliefs. Facts can inform your practice and interaction for the better and can shed light on how you might equitably approach working with the client. For example, being familiar with the dos and don'ts of a given culture can also help you adjust in a way that is respectful of your client (McDougal-Miller & O'Callaghan, 2010). With regard to cultural norms, be aware that the degree to which your client does or does not ascribe will vary as their unique identity or intersectionality cannot be predicted. It is for these reasons that you must be open to learning about your client's culture and how they perceive and express their identity (Adams, 2004; Chase, 2003; Valentino, 2006; Walker, 2004). One resource to consider is the book *Cultural Intersections in Music Therapy: Music, Health, and the Person*, edited by Annette Whitehead-Pleaux and Xueli Tan (2017). Among other topics, the book details cultures of heritage, religion, sexual orientation, gender, disability, and survivorship.

> *Food for thought:* Building rapport can be easier when we are among people of a familiar culture, and interacting around music that is familiar. However, how do you proceed when those elements aren't present for you in a music therapy session?

Even musically speaking, with regard to preferences, there are several things to consider when treatment planning such as, a) the person's background, b) where they grew up, c) the types of cultural and musical influences that were around them, d) the styles they gravitate towards, and in some cases, e) the role of assimilation and integration in a person's life (Certification Board for Music Therapists, 2020; Kim & Whitehead-Pleaux, 2015; Whitehead-Pleaux, Brink, & Tan, 2017). For example, over time I came to notice that my older clients who liked Christian music typically preferred hymns. During an assessment with a couple in their 70s, I wrongfully assumed that they liked hymns when they mentioned a love of Christian music.

To my surprise, they preferred current, contemporary Christian songs. Their preferred music was the result of the styles they had been exposed to through the contemporary services at their place of worship. That encounter reminded me not to assume even when I've been able to identify a trend among patients, because it won't apply to everyone.

Client-preferred music

Particularly in the music therapy setting, "…a therapist's awareness of his/her own ethnic identity should include reflection upon his/her musical biases and preferences" (Valentino, 2006). While it is okay to introduce new music to a client, it should not be used exclusively in place of your client's preferred music. This is because it is important, within the context of the therapeutic relationship, to utilize the patient's preferred music in session (Hinman, 2010; Silverman, Letwin & Neuhring, 2016; Standley, 1986; Valentino, 2006). In some instances, it's actually recommended that therapists only use other types of music after building rapport incorporating the client's preferred music first (Silverman, 2019). Studies on the use of patient-preferred music (live and pre-recorded) show its efficacy with regard to multiple goal areas in the medical setting, including psychosocial needs (Crawford, Hogan, & Silverman, 2013; Hogan & Silverman, 2015; Madson & Silverman, 2010; Mitchell & MacDonald, 2006).

CASE EXAMPLE: STUCK BETWEEN WORLDS

To the outside world, this patient and I were both black, but, beyond race, our cultures were very different. It was early in my career, and the level of disclosure that I was used to from my patients wasn't there in this case. I found myself questioning my effectiveness as a therapist. With this patient, music played a primary role in the session whereas with most others, there would be a mix of music, verbal processing, and emotional expression. In the medical setting, most of the patients I encountered were primarily low-context communicators—they spoke directly and were relatively open even on first encounter; what they said was exactly what they meant, without the need for interpretation (Croucher, et al., 2012; Sue & Sue, 2016). At the same time, while still expressive and highly communicative, some patients incorporate aspects of high-context communication, using euphemisms to avoid naming their diagnosis or reporting on aspects of their prognosis in a cryptic manner, requiring me to interpret the hidden meaning and deeper context behind what was said (Croucher, *et al.*, 2012; Nam, 2015; Sue & Sue, 2016).

With this particular patient, though she exuded a gentle kindness, my interactions with her were met with brief, generalized answers; she was reserved. Her responses were sometimes direct, though closed-ended in a way that I would later learn alluded to high-context content that I was ill-equipped to interpret and unaware of at times. During musical moments which were largely receptive methods, she would sometimes close her eyes and lean her head back into the tall chair. At other times, she would fix her gaze at a point across the room. After the music, a calm, quiet "thank you" broke the silence and she asked me to return during her next treatment. I did so. And at her request, I did so again the next time. On one occasion when I let her know I was going to be away on the date of her next session, to my surprise she said, "No, you can't take time off when I'm going to be here!" Though lighthearted in manner, the patient communicated both understanding and disappointment in that moment. It clued me in that there was more going on therapeutically than I was able to perceive initially. In hindsight, the scope of my assessment had been narrowed in a way that hampered me when presented with this patient whose culture and communication style was different from that I was used to.

In the session following my absence, the patient stated that she had really missed having a session. Over time, I came to know a little bit more about her life and work in the general sense, though our sessions remained music focused and receptive in nature. With patient-preferred live music as the central experience in sessions, I later realized that the autonomy the patient established in the song selection decision-making process was therapeutic in and of itself, with song choices also serving as forms of communication and expression for the patient (Dileo, 2000; Silverman, 2019).

One day, something the patient mentioned about her children made me ask a clarifying question about their level of awareness about her disease. Her response shed light on an internal conflict she was having. In a distressed manner the patient stated, "My kids don't even know. They see my hair falling out and they know I'm sick, but my husband says no. Our native culture is very private, but I told him we are in the United States now…he insists no, though. My cousin also had cancer and my kids are asking questions because they saw what happened to her…but I can't tell them…"

In that moment, for the first time, I came to understand that her reserved demeanor was a facet of her cultural identity, and what she shared from session to session was to her degree of comfort and according to her cultural norms. I realized that I had been evaluating her and the efficacy of my work based on a measurement that did not identify or acknowledge her cultural identity. If she wasn't able to speak openly with her children, who was I to think that she should open up to me, a stranger? At the same time, I was thankful that we reached a point in our therapeutic relationship that she felt comfortable enough to express herself so deeply (Davis, Gfeller, & Thaut, 2008).

Study question

1. What are some ways that you can assess a client's progress when their communication style differs from your typical benchmarks?

In their article on musical multicultural competency, Hadley and Norris (2016) share that "through human socialization, both implicit and/or explicit, individuals learn what their outer world deems as important, relevant, valuable, acceptable, and/or normative" (p.131). Conflict can be present when one's outer world changes, leaving the person to figure out if they will adapt, as well and how and to what degree. Of note, is that this process is non-linear, and can be ever-evolving. The patient in the case study above certainly had a change in her outer world between her home country and the United States. Though she had a desire to adopt certain aspects of the more liberal American culture, the client's husband believed in maintaining the norms of their native culture. Within the private and patriarchal nature of her native culture, she was ultimately unable to be open with her children. However, the trust built over time in the music therapy setting enabled the patient to open up to me when needed (Potvin, Bradt, & Kesslick, 2015).

Since then, I've had many other instances where identifying the client's culture helped me to better assess, meet needs, and co-construct the therapeutic relationship (Dileo, 2000). In turn, this has enabled clients to verbalize needs when comfortable and as needed, and it beneficially challenges me to actively listen, observe, and understand the variety of ways clients communicate their needs (Kim & Whitehead-Pleaux, 2015; McDougal-Miller & O'Callaghan, 2010).

CASE EXAMPLE: MEXICAN MUSIC/ SPANISH-LANGUAGE OFFERING

I remember encountering a patient on his first day of chemotherapy who had multiple family members present. After introducing music therapy services, the patient exclaimed, "If you don't know any Mexican songs, I don't want it!" In that moment, I found myself quickly thinking through my repertoire. I knew some songs that were in Spanish, but with the specificity of his request, I didn't want to make assumptions about the national origin of those songs' artists. My approach was to make the distinction and inform him that I knew some Spanish-language songs. He said, "Oh, I was just kidding, but what do you know?" The first name I called out was the Mexican-American singer Selena. To the one-word name the client responded, "Who, Selena Gomez?" and began to laugh with a relative. I clarified, pronouncing the singer's name as it would be spoken in Spanish. The patient exclaimed, "Oh, SELENAS! Why didn't you just say that?"

Next, he inquired about my knowledge of west coast rap: "Do you know any Ice Cube or Snoop Dogg?" I was familiar with the music of both artists, but had never attempted either on acoustic guitar or used it in session before. I was up for the challenge though, so I quickly searched to find comparable chords and sang the chorus to one of Snoop's songs. The client was ecstatic. He relaxed back into his chair; I had passed his test. From there, he asked for me to sing a Selena song. After the song, he and his brother reminisced and were easy to engage in the music therapy session. When his parents returned, he asked that I share the Selena song again.

Before bringing that initial session to a close, I took time to ask the patient more about his musical preferences, including favorite Mexican songs and artists. As he named artists and genres that I was unfamiliar with, I took note (Baker, 2014). The exercise became a family activity and at times became a jovial debate as to which songs were the best for whom, and why.

During that initial assessment session, which was also the patient's first treatment, he also identified and communicated to his mother which song he wanted played at his funeral and why, translating the theme of the song into English for me. With an unknown prognosis, it was powerful to see the patient discuss his own mortality and communicate aspects of his final wishes through the context of song preference in the music therapy setting. With the patient and family requesting follow-up, knowledge of his preferred music helped me to prepare for future sessions.

Study questions

1. What types of cultural dynamics were present?

2. What interpersonal dynamics were present?

3. What other approaches could you take to effectively work with a patient whose musical preferences are outside what you are familiar with?

Chapter discussion

We will all come across clients and patients of another culture, even if we are the same ethnicity. How can we prepare to work with them successfully, particularly in a first session when we don't have access to background information before we enter the session? What type of approach, techniques, and ways of being can we employ to help us serve our clients?

Things to remember— the therapeutic exchange:

- Create an environment where you can continually learn about the client (their point of view, culture, etc.).

- Connect on the sameness, acknowledge the differences (the latter is not always a verbal process).

- Keep your therapeutic goal in mind.

- Be a student and the facilitator, exhibiting an openness to learn and guide.

Food for thought: Think about equity as part of this process, being in partnership with the patient as well as honoring patient agency.

Music

As music therapists, we will encounter a wide variety of clients throughout our career. Since "no single style of music will be valued by all people," it is imperative that our musical repertoire is eclectic enough to serve all of our clients (American Music Therapy Association, 2013; Certification Board for Music Therapists, 2020; Davis, Gfeller, & Thaut, 2008, p.69). This section will provide tips, techniques and insights for you to keep in mind as you build your own musical repertoire.

Pre-section discussions

You've just learned that your next music therapy site is going to be at a cancer center where the patient age range is 20–90, with a median age of 50 years old. The patients vary in terms of race, ethnicity, socio-economic status, and level of education.

What steps can you take to build an intentional and varied repertoire of songs for use in music therapy sessions where the target goal is to provide psychosocial support to adult patients?

In an online search, what keywords would you use and why?

Building repertoire intentionally

For many of us, it was our love of music, in part, that led us to the field of music therapy. Even when you are well into your professional years, I encourage you to continue to be a student of music—not just technically with skill, but also with the depth and breadth of your musical knowledge (Silverman, 2019). As a start, be sure to expand beyond the music you grew up with and typically listen to. As you delve into genres outside your foundational knowledge base, think about the following: "What makes the art form the art form?" Of note is that genres are broad categories that can be broken down by style into smaller, more specific subgenres. For example, if a client likes hip-hop, that information is only a broad entry point into determining that aspect of their musical preferences, as the genre is so vast (Reed & Brooks, 2017). For a more complete picture, you'll need to retrieve more information about their preferred artists, songs, eras, and style(s) of hip-hop.

Learning a new song is much more than reading the sheet music or a lead sheet and memorizing what is on the page. Is there a particular strum pattern, feel or vocal styling that makes the genre what it is? How can you stay true to those elements when learning and when playing the song live? Care and consideration should also be taken to preserve the integrity of the style through study of the original recordings. For instance, when playing a reggae song, implementing a reggae strum accenting the offbeat (the "and" of each beat) is advised for authenticity, rather than using a generic strum that emphasizes the "1" as the down beat like many standard American tunes do. Other aspects to consider are themes—what emotions, feelings, or imagery does the song tend to evoke? What themes are contained in the lyrical content? A working knowledge of all these will come in handy when needing to select music to match or evoke a particular mood or sentiment in the session.

Adding to your repertoire can seem like a daunting task, but as a starting point, you can begin by familiarizing yourself with the prominent styles in your region, also considering cultural and ethnic issues. Are there lyrics you should omit from a song as a non-native of that culture? Are certain types of music used religiously or ceremonially to the degree that it would be inappropriate to bring them into a session (Chase, 2003; Hahna, 2017)? In the case of music from another culture, when you don't have access to someone native to that culture, online resources may be helpful, granted you carefully curate sources and verify. You can also look into workshops, webinars or other online content.

Pop culture

For a deeper analysis, when learning new music and familiarizing yourself with the artists and eras, also pay attention to any applicable elements of pop culture and history. Your client may have personal connections to the time period or music that you can utilize in session if you are aware of this history. For example, beyond the music:

- Cyndi Lauper was a 1980s pop culture icon and influencer when it came to fashion and inspiring women and girls.

- In the 1960s, much of the folk music was comprised of protest songs during the Vietnam War. At the same time, Beatlemania, the term coined to signify the massive popularity and fan hysteria of the Beatles, prompted the British Invasion in the US, where UK bands such as The Rolling Stones, The Who, and The Animals rose to fame (Robbins, 2018).

Having this knowledge strengthens your musical expertise and adds to the possible points of connection available to build rapport with your client.

Decades

Beyond genre, song selection can be informed by the patient's preferred decade(s) of music. This makes it important to be able to categorize your music by decade and recall that information in session. When expanding your musical repertoire, you can add in popular songs from the range of decades that are pertinent to the population(s) you are working with.

Geographical relevance

Finding out where your client is from may clue you into what types of regional music they may like. For example, a patient originally from New Jersey, who is seeking treatment in Texas may like Billy Joel and Bruce Springsteen (artists from the north east who are very popular in that area) over Willie Nelson (a native Texan whose music is very popular in the South). While all are well known artists, their music is a staple in different parts of the US, coinciding with their regions of residence and the stylistic sounds most popular in those areas. While we can't take these cultural notions as absolutes, we can utilize them as guideposts when needed, to be verified in dialogue with the client.

Practicing in the state of Texas, I find that many clients like country music, but as mentioned earlier with the hip-hop example, the specific type of preferred music within the broad genre can vary greatly. Some clients' musical preferences are influenced by what was popular with their parents or grandparents, while others prefer the music from their own era or that of their children. Geography can also play a large role, based on who and what styles are popular in that region (Kim & Whitehead-Pleaux, 2015).

For example, since moving to Texas from the north east, I have come to learn a lot more about country and western music. There are certain niche styles of country like red dirt music specific to Oklahoma and North Texas, and truck-driving country that encompasses lifestyle songs about the truck-driving industry. Both of those genres sound very different from the contemporary and pop-influenced country music styles I had previously used to define the whole genre. As it applies to the clinical setting, consulting the client to draw out the details of their preferences is always advised and can offer valuable insight about the client, based on the nature of their preferences and the ways in which they speak about them.

Food for thought: If a patient likes a certain artist, what does that indicate about the era, genre, and possible similar artists and styles of music that they may also like?

Exercise:

- Working in pairs, write down the names of three

popular musical artists or groups, ensuring that a variety of time periods and genres are represented.

• Now trade papers and write down the genre, time period, and two to three similar artists or groups for each name listed.

This will help you to broaden your knowledge base of music, so that if you are in a situation where a patient says they like James Taylor, for example, but you don't know how to play any of his songs, you might at least know that he was a folk-rock-style artist who rose to prominence during the 1970s singer-songwriter era (Encyclopedia Britannica, 2018). You could think about what 1970s folk or similar style of music you know of to use in the session instead.

In a clinical setting, this type of information also helps you to get a picture of the patient's likes and dislikes, based on their thoughts about similar artists, enabling you to get a deeper sense of their musical tastes. Having this knowledge is especially helpful during your first encounter with a patient where they may feel "put on the spot" or otherwise unprepared to think of their musical preferences. In seeking to enable success for the patient, being able to quell potential feelings of inadequacy by providing a springboard for the patient to choose from, and/or be supported by, is essential when it comes to learning about their preferred music and artists.

Initial encounters

If you find that you are completely unfamiliar with your client's preferred music, but are already in session, how can you utilize their expertise to learn more about it from or with them?

• Inquire about the style, the history, and key artists that define the genre. Sometimes the patient will know those levels of detail and take great delight in the opportunity to share them. In other instances, it is best to ask direct, yet open-ended questions to guide the conversation:

- "Who should I search for?"

- "Who is popular in that style?"

- "Who are your favorite groups? Why?"

Any time you have a series of questions to ask a client, be sure to pace yourself rather than ask the questions in immediate succession. This method leaves room for natural dialogue and for the patient to elaborate or reflect as desired. Keep in mind that your questions are a starting point for active listening and learning, rather than a one-dimensional checklist to get through in order to determine next steps. The difference in approach is the difference between the interaction feeling like a conversation, or just a one-dimensional interview for the client. When it comes to building rapport, the former is a stronger tool than the latter. It is the development of your therapeutic skills that will enable you to more easily facilitate discussion, while recognizing and adapting to evolving patient needs in a session.

- If age-appropriate for patient and song era (at least 20 years ago, granted they were adults or at least teens at that time), ask "What were times like when this music was first popular?" This can serve as a tool for reminiscence and information gathering. If the client/caregiver isn't so familiar with those details, guide the conversation in a way that they can still contribute without feeling pressure to recall. This is why it's important to figure out how people consume music early on in the session and to determine their relationship with it. Some will know a lot of details down to band history, while others may just know what they like when they hear it, without ever paying particular attention to the artist.

While you can write down the information shared with you for future reference, there is an additional option:

- Use an internet-connected tablet computer such as an iPad to explore patient suggestions in real time, engaging the client in a music listening experience. As you are listening, regardless of your personal opinion of the song, ask yourself the following:

- "What aspects of the music—lyrics, musicality, function, philosophy, style—can I appreciate?"

- "What points of connection can I find?" You want to be genuine, listen openly, and, if nothing else, know that you gained a deeper understanding of the patient and their music.

As the client is listening, also observe them. Are there shifts in their temperament, facial expression or body language? What effect did the song have on them? Supplemental questions can help you learn more about the patient as well. Additionally, showing a genuine interest in learning more about your client and the music that is meaningful to them can be very beneficial towards building rapport (Baker, 2014).

You can ask the following to gain more insight into the client's perspective:

- What was it like to listen to this music in this moment?

- What initially drew you to this music?

  - How did you first get introduced to this music?

- What has kept you listening to this group/music over the years?

  - What do you like about the music/the artist/group?

All things considered, introducing music as the mutual "friend" and showing consideration enough to incorporate the music that they're already connected to can help you to build rapport by association. When you do that, you've integrated a mutual "friend" whom the client already knows and likes. As you gather information and familiarize yourself with the client's preferred music, you may be able to draw from your own repertoire as well, to introduce the client to new music that resonates with themes and elements of their preferred music and clinical needs area(s) (McDougal-Miller & O'Callaghan, 2010).

Summary

Music, culture, and interpersonal relations are vast and complex subjects interwoven into the very fabric of music therapy practice. At the same time, while cultural considerations are spoken about, they have not been fully integrated into the field. As expressions of culture, preferred music and styles of communication vary between clients; it is important to exercise cultural humility over cultural competence.

This chapter was designed to be an informational springboard to inspire further research, reflection, and preparation as it pertains to building rapport and addressing the psychosocial needs areas of culturally diverse adult clients. Though the entry-level curriculum in our field does not currently teach cultural humility as a standard part of music therapy programs across the US at this point in time, it is my hope that not only will that change, but that over time, more students and therapists will be aware of, open to and *do* the individual work required to help our field become more inclusive, and equipped to serve everyone equitably.

References

Adams, R. (2004). "The Five Good Things in Cross-Cultural Therapy." In M. Walker & W. B. Rosen (eds), How *Connections Heal: Stories from Relational-Cultural Therapy*. New York, NY: Guilford Press.

American Music Therapy Association. (2013). *Professional Competencies*. Retrieved from www.musictherapy.org/about/competencies.

American Music Therapy Association. (2019). *Code of Ethics*. Retrieved from www.musictherapy.org/about/ethics.

American Music Therapy Association. (n.d.). A Career in Music Therapy. Retrieved from www.musictherapy.org/careers/employment/#PERSONAL_QUALIFICATIONS.

Arthur, M. H. (2018). "A humanistic perspective on intersubjectivity in music psychotherapy." *Music Therapy Perspectives*, 2(36), 161–167. doi: https://doi.org/10.1093/mtp/miy017.

Baker, F. (2014). "An investigation of the sociocultural factors impacting on the therapeutic songwriting process." *Nordic Journal of Music Therapy*, 2(23), 123–151. http://dx.doi.org/10.1080/08098131.2013.783094.

Birnbaum, J. (2014). "Intersubjectivity and Nordoff-Robbins Music Therapy." *Music Therapy Perspectives*, 32(1), 30–37. 10.1093/mtp/miu004.

Bolger, L., McFerran, K. S., & Stige, B. (2018). "Hanging out and buying in: Rethinking relationship building to avoid tokenism when striving for collaboration in music therapy." *Music Therapy Perspectives*, 2(36), 257–266. https://doi.org/10.1093/mtp/miy002.

Borzcon, R. (2004). *Music Therapy: A Fieldwork Primer*. Gilsum, NH: Barcelona Publishers.

Brescia, T. (2005). "A qualitative study of intuition as experienced and used by music therapists." *Qualitative Inquiries in Music Therapy*, 2, 62–112.

Brunell, A. (2007). "Self-Disclosure." In R. F. Baumeister & K. D. Vohs (eds), *Encyclopedia of Social Psychology, 1*, (pp.811–812). doi: 10.4135/9781412956253. n482.

Bruscia, K. (ed.) (1998). *The Dynamics of Music Psychotherapy*. Gilsum, NH: Barcelona Publishers.

Bruscia, K. (1989). "The practical side of improvisational music therapy." *Music Therapy Perspectives*, 1(6), 11–15. https://doi.org/10.1093/mtp/6.1.11. Bottom of Form.

Certification Board for Music Therapists. (2015). *Board Certification Domains*. Retrieved from www.cbmt.org/upload/CBMT_Board_Certification_Domains_2015.pdf.

Certification Board for Music Therapists. (2020). *Board Certification Domains*. Retrieved from www.cbmt.org/wp-content/uploads/2020/03/CBMT_Board_Certification_Domains_2020.pdf.

Chase, K. (2003). "Multicultural music therapy: A review of literature." *Music Therapy Perspectives*, 21(2), 84–88. doi:10.1093/mtp/21.2.84.

Cormier, S. L. & Hackney, H. (2008). *Counseling Strategies and Interventions*. Newmarket, Ontario, Canada: Allyn & Bacon.

Cormier, S. L., Nurius, P., & Osborn, C. J. (2009). *Interviewing and Change Strategies for Helpers: Fundamental Skills and Cognitive Behavioral Interventions*. Belmont, CA: Brooks/Cole.

Crawford, I., Hogan, T., & Silverman, M. J. (2013). "Effects of music therapy on perception of stress, relaxation, mood, and side effects in patients on a solid organ transplant unit: A randomized effectiveness study." *The Arts in Psychotherapy*, 40(2), 224–229. doi:10.1016/j.aip.2013.02.005.

Croucher, S. M., Bruno, A., McGrath, P., Adams, C., McGahan. C, Suits, A., & Huckins, A. (2012). "Conflict styles and high–low context cultures: A cross-cultural extension." *Communication Research Reports*, 1(29), 64–73.

Culture (n.d). In *Cambridge Business English Dictionary*. Retrieved from https://dictionary.cambridge.org/us/dictionary/english/culture.

Curtis, S. (2017). "Intersections of Gender and Culture." In A. Whitehead-Pleaux & X. Tan (Eds.), *Cultural Intersections in Music Therapy* (pp.207–222). Gilsum, NH: Barcelona Publishers.

Darrow, A.A., & Johnson, C. (2009). "Preservice music teachers' and therapists' nonverbal behaviors and their relationship to perceived rapport." *International Journal of Music Education*, 27(3), 269–280. https://doi.org/10.1177/0255761409337276.

Davis, W. B., Gfeller, K. E., & Thaut, M. H. (2008). *An Introduction to Music Therapy: Theory and Practice*. Silver Springs, MD: American Music Therapy Association.

Dileo, C. (2000). *Ethical Thinking in Music Therapy*. Cherry Hill, NJ: Jeffrey Books.

Encyclopedia Britannica. (2018). James Taylor. Retrieved from www. britannica.com/biography/James-Taylor.

Gallardo, M. E., Yeh, C. J., Trimble, J. E., & Parham, T. A. (2012). *Culturally Adaptive Counseling Skills: Demonstrations of Evidence-Based Practices*. Thousand Oaks, CA: Sage Publications. doi: 10.4135/9781483349329.

Genre (n.d.). In *Merriam-Webster's Online Dictionary*. Retrieved from www. merriam-webster.com/dictionary/genre.

Grocke, D. E. & Wigram, T. (2007). *Receptive Methods in Music Therapy: Techniques and Clinical Applications for Music Therapy Clinicians, Educators, and Students*. London, UK and Philadelphia, PA: Jessica Kingsley Publishers.

Hadley, S. (2017). "I Don't See You as Black/Gay/Disabled/Muslim/etc.: Microaggressions in Everyday Encounters." In A. Whitehead-Pleaux & X. Tan (eds), *Cultural Intersections in Music Therapy: Music, Health, and the Person* (pp.11–22). Gilsum, NH: Barcelona Publishers.

Hadley, S. & Norris, M. S. (2016). "Musical multicultural competency in music therapy: The first step." *Music Therapy Perspectives*, 34(2), 129–137. doi:10.1093/mtp/miv045.

Hahna, N. D. (2017). "Reflecting on Personal Bias." In A. Whitehead-Pleaux & X. Tan (eds), *Cultural Intersections in Music Therapy: Music, Health, and the Person* (pp.23–33). Gilsum, NH: Barcelona Publishers.

Hanser, S. (1999) *New Music Therapist's Handbook* (second edition). Boston, MA: Berklee Press.

Hinman, M. L. (2010). "Our song: Music therapy with couples when one partner is medically hospitalized." *Music Therapy Perspectives*, 28(1), 29–36. Retrieved from http://search.ebscohost.com.ezp.twu.edu/login.aspx?d irect=true&db=ccm&AN=105096679&site=ehost-live.

Hogan, T. & Silverman, M. J. (2015). "Coping-infused dialogue through patient-preferred live music: A medical music therapy protocol and randomized pilot study for hospitalized organ transplant patients." *Journal of Music Therapy*, 52(3), 420–436. doi:10.15640/ijmpa.v4n2a2

Intersubjectivity. (2009). In A. S. Reber, R. Allen, & E. S. Reber (eds), *The Penguin Dictionary of Psychology* (fourth edition). London, UK: Penguin.

Jones, C., Baker, F., & Day, T. (2004). "From healing rituals to music therapy: Bridging the cultural divide between therapist and young Sudanese refugees." *The Arts in Psychotherapy*, 31, 89–100. doi:10.1016/j. aip.2004.02.002.

Kim, S. & Whitehead-Pleaux, A. (2015). "Music Therapy and Cultural Diversity." In B. L. Wheeler (ed.). *Music Therapy Handbook* (pp.51–63). New York, NY: Guilford Press.

Kumagai, A. K. & Lypson, M. L. (2009). "Beyond cultural competence: Critical consciousness, social justice, and multicultural education." *Academic Medicine*, 84(6), 782–787. doi: 10.1097/ACM.0b013e3181a42398.

Leach, M. J. (2005). "Rapport: A key to treatment success." *Complementary Therapies in Clinical Practice*, 11(4), 262–265.

Madson, A. & Silverman, M. J. (2010). "The effect of music therapy on relaxation, anxiety, pain perception, and nausea in adult solid organ transplant patients." *Journal of Music Therapy*, 47(3), 220–232. doi:10.1093/jmt/47.3.220.

McDougal-Miller, D. & O'Callaghan, C. (2010). "Cancer Care." In D. Hanson-Abromeit & C. Colwell (eds.), *Effective Clinical Practice in Music Therapy: Medical Music Therapy for Adults in Hospital Settings* (pp.217–306). Silver Spring, MD: American Music Therapy Association.

Mitchell, L. A. & Macdonald, R. A. R. (2006). "An experimental investigation of the effects of preferred and relaxing music listening on pain perception." *Journal of Music Therapy*, 43(4), 295–316. https://doi-org.ezp.twu.edu/10.1093/jmt/43.4.295.

Nam, K. A. (2015). "High-Context and Low-Context Communication." In J. M. Bennett (ed.), *The SAGE Encyclopedia of Intercultural Competence* (first edition) (pp.377–381). Thousand Oaks, CA: Sage Publications. Retrieved from www.researchgate.net/figure/Low-Context-High-Context-Communication_Bl1_280948728.

Páez, M. & Albert, L. (2012). "Cultural Consciousness." In J. A. Banks (ed.), *Encyclopedia of Diversity in Education* (Vol. 1, pp.510–510). Thousand Oaks, CA: Sage Publications. doi: 10.4135/9781452218533.n160.

Patallo, B. J. (2019). "The multicultural guidelines in practice: Cultural humility in clinical training and supervision." *Training and Education in Professional Psychology*, 13(3), 227–232. https://doi.org/10.1037/tep0000253.

Pieterse, A. L., Lee, M, Ritmeester, A., & Collins, N. M. (2013) "Towards a model of self-awareness development for counselling and psychotherapy training." *Counselling Psychology Quarterly*, 26(2), 190–207, doi: 10.1080/09515070.2013.793451.

Potvin, N., Bradt, J., & Kesslick, A. (2015). "Expanding perspective on music therapy for symptom management in cancer care." *Journal of Music Therapy*, 52(1), 135–167. doi:10.1093/jmt/thu056.

Rafieyan, R. (2017). "32 Flavors (and Then Some): Reflections on Identities That Fall Somewhere in Between." In A. Whitehead-Pleaux & X. Tan (eds), *Cultural Intersections in Music Therapy: Music, Health, and the Person* (pp.137–151). Gilsum, NH: Barcelona Publishers.

Rapport. (n.d.). In *Farlex Partner Medical Dictionary*. Retrieved from https://medical-dictionary.thefreedictionary.com/rapport.

Reed, K. J. & Brooks, D. (2017). "African-American Perspectives." In A. Whitehead-Pleaux & X. Tan (eds), *Cultural Intersections in Music Therapy: Music, Health, and the Person* (pp.105–123). Gilsum, NH: Barcelona Publishers.

Riess, H. (2017). "The science of empathy." *Journal of Patient Experience*. Retrieved from https://journals.sagepub.com/doi/10.1177/2374373517699267.

Robbins, I. A. (2018). British Invasion. *Encyclopedia Britannica*. Retrieved from www.britannica.com/event/British-Invasion.

Rolvsjord, R. (2009). *Resource-Oriented Music Therapy in Mental Health Care*. Gilsum, NH: Barcelona Publishers.

Rolvsjord, R. (2016). "Five episodes of clients' contributions to the therapeutic relationship: A qualitative study in adult mental health care." *Nordic Journal of Music Therapy*, 25(2), 159–184. doi: 10.1080/08098131.2015.1010562.

Sadovnik, N. (2016). "Shira chadasha: A new song for an old community." *Music Therapy Perspectives*, 34(2), 147–153. doi: https://doi.org/10.1093/mtp/miw015.

Scheiby, B. B. (2005). "An intersubjective approach to music therapy: Identification and processing of musical countertransference in a music psychotherapeutic context." *Music Therapy Perspectives*, 23(1), 8–17. doi:10.1093/mtp/23.1.8.

Silverman, M. J. (2019). "Music therapy and therapeutic alliance in adult mental health: A qualitative investigation." *Journal of Music Therapy*, 56(1), 90–116doi:10.1093/jmt/thy019.

Silverman, M. J., Letwin, L., & Nuehring, L. (2016). "Patient preferred live music with adult medical patients: A systematic review to determine implications for clinical practice and future research." *Arts in Psychotherapy*, 49, 1–7. https://doi.org/10.1016/j.aip.2016.05.004.

Standley, J. M. (1986). "Music research in medical/dental treatment: Meta-analysis and clinical applications." *Journal of Music Therapy*, 23(2), 56–122. https://doi.org/10.1093/jmt/23.2.56.

Sue, D. W. & Sue, D. (2016). *Counseling the Culturally Diverse: Theory & Practice*. Hoboken, NJ. John Wiley & Sons.

Teniente, S. F. & Guerra, N. S. (2011). "Active Listening." In S. Goldstein & J. A. Naglieri (eds), *Encyclopedia of Child Behavior and Development* (pp.27–28). Boston, MA: Springer US. doi:10.1007/978-0-387-79061-9_47.

Tervalon, M. & Murray-Garcia, J. (1998). "Cultural humility vs cultural competence: A critical distinction in defining physician training outcomes in medical education." *Journal of Health Care for the Poor and Underserved*, 9(2), 117–125.

Trondalen, G. (2019). "Musical intersubjectivity." *The Arts in Psychotherapy*, 65, 1–6.

Upshaw, N. C., Lewis, D. E. Jr., & Nelson, A, L. (2019). "Cultural humility in action: Reflective and process-oriented supervision with black trainees." *Training and Education in Professional Psychology*. Advance online publication. doi: 10.1037/tep0000284.

U.S. Census Bureau. (2018, July 1). Most Populous Cities. U.S. Census Bureau, Population Division.

Valentino, R. E. (2006). "Attitudes towards cross-cultural empathy in music therapy." *Music Therapy Perspectives*, 24(2), 108–114. Validation. (n.d.). In

Oxford Living Dictionary. Retrieved from https://en.oxforddictionaries. com/definition/validation.

Walker, M. (2004). "Walking a Piece of the Way: Race, Power, and Therapeutic Movement." In M. Walker & W. B. Rosen (eds), *How Connections Heal: Stories from Relational-Cultural Therapy.* New York, NY: Guilford Press.

Whitehead-Pleaux, A., Brink, S. L., & Tan, X. (2017). "Culturally Competent Music Therapy Assessments." In A. Whitehead-Pleaux & X. Tan (eds.), *Cultural Intersections in Music Therapy: Music, Health, and the Person* (pp.271–283). Gilsum, NH: Barcelona Publishers.

Williams, K. & Abad, V. (2005). "Reflections on music therapy with indigenous families: Cultural learning put into practice." *Australian Journal of Music Therapy,* 16, 60–69.

Williams, M. A. (2001). *The 10 Lenses: Your Guide to Living & Working in a Multicultural World.* Sterling, VA: Capital Books.

Wilson, J., Ward, C., & Fischer, R. (2013). "Beyond culture learning theory: What can personality tell us about cultural competence?" *Journal of Cross-Cultural Psychology,* 44(6), 900–927. https://doi.org/10.1177/0022022113492889.

CHAPTER 3

LGBTQ+ Music Therapy

BETH ROBINSON, MT-BC

LEAH OSWANSKI, MA, LPC, MT-BC

Beth: *I have been called: "it," "faggot," "dyke," and "disgusting" among other slurs. I have been told to act more feminine, told to stop pretending to be a man. I have been told I was going to hell, that I was ruining my life, and that I was ruining other people's lives, that I was hurting my family and community. I have been told I would amount to nothing and would drop out of college. That I could end up dead from being murdered or from contracting AIDS or from a drug overdose. I have been threatened. I have been physically assaulted. I have had the windows of my car smashed and a chair thrown at my head. I have been told that the discrimination I received was my fault because I had chosen my "lifestyle." I have experienced teachers, professors, friends, and colleagues turn their backs on me and remain silent when I was facing discrimination. I have been made to feel less-than, subhuman, and broken.*

All these life experiences had to do with one thing: being LGBTQ+.

The above examples happened within my first ten years of coming out between the years 1990 and 2000, during my music therapy schooling and first years working as a music therapist. Some of these experiences and messages came from people I loved and trusted: family members, friends, and teachers. Some messages came from society and media: TV shows, news, local and federal government, school and college, and organized religion. While this happens to be my personal story and experience, it is not so unique within the LGBTQ+ community. Everyone in the LGBTQ+ community experiences some level of discrimination and is subject to microaggressions in their lives.

I identify as LGBTQ+, as a gender queer pansexual person who has been out in some form since my teen years. I finished my internship, passed my boards and received my BA in music therapy in 1996 and began working as a music therapist the same year. Today, I still continue to work as a music therapist as well as run a music therapy business in the Bay Area. Remembering back to my life as a young queer music therapy student in the 1990s, I can honestly say that I did not feel seen or supported by my professors or supervisors. Nor did I have any education on working with LGBTQ+ clients. There was no education or discussion about LGBTQ+ culture, topics, history or people in the music therapy curriculum. It was as if we would never meet or work with an LGBTQ+ person in a clinical setting. Or if we did, that their sexuality and gender were not important.

While there was not much overt homophobia or transphobia in my music therapy education, what I did experience were constant microaggressions, invisibility, heteronormativity and minimizing of the LGBTQ+ existence. "What happens in your bedroom is not business of mine," "I don't care who you love, I just don't want to see it" and similar sayings were commonplace during this time and it was usually said to convey acceptance or tolerance toward LGBTQ+ people. As if it was only the act of sex that identified that person as LGBTQ+ and if we just didn't discuss that…POOF…suddenly we are all the same!

This is similar to statements like: "I don't see color" when discussing race. That statement is often said to convey acceptance but basically communicates, "I don't see you." LGBTQ+ people have different lived experiences from heterosexual cisgendered people, just as people of color have different lived experiences from white people. If you don't acknowledge that, you are not acknowledging the existence of that person. There is more to an LGBTQ+ person than just who they are having sex with. There is more to a transgender (T) person than their gender. There is a lifetime of unique experiences and LGBTQ+ culture that they are part of.

While I will never experience the privilege of living a life free of discrimination, in 2019 I do live a life demonstrating more acceptance, understanding and protections than 20 years ago. This positive progression has come from macro levels of change, including federal and state laws, a level of societal acceptance, and healthier LGBTQ+

representation in the media and society. There are also micro levels of change within schools, places of employment, and communities. Living in California, I have the right to marry, the right to start a family and have child custody. There are anti-discrimination and hate crime laws in place that help protect me from being assaulted, fired, being refused housing, or healthcare here. Unfortunately, many of these laws are state laws, which are offered in only a few of the states in America. Protections and laws can be stripped away quickly, as we have seen during the Trump administration.

The LGBTQ+ community is rich and diverse and part of our larger American society. LGBTQ+ people come in all ethnic backgrounds, socio-economic backgrounds, all religious backgrounds, all ages, and all genders. My interest and passion in writing about LGBTQ+ topics are to keep visibility and education progressing. With this chapter, I hope to create more visibility for LGBTQ+ people and culture in the music therapy setting. To invite conversations and discussions about LGBTQ+-related topics into the classroom. To challenge students and educators to acknowledge and unpack bias they might have toward the LGBTQ+ community, understand what unique challenges and stressors LGBTQ+ people are facing as a minority, and deepen students and educators' awareness of how to become better allies for the LGBTQ+ community.

Leah: I sat down to write the personal story for this chapter and I stared at the screen blankly for what seemed like hours. How do I write from a vulnerable place as to why this topic is important to me while balancing my role in oppression with my experience of being oppressed? How do I share my experiences without getting caught in the trap of internalized phobias and "isms" that I battle? How can I do all this without exposing my personal life to you, most of whom are strangers to me? That's the weird thing about being LGBTQ+. In order to have conversations about our marginalized identities, we may have to share very private information to help people have a frame of reference. Another weird thing for me about being LGBTQ+ is that my privilege is fluid and depends on the gender (or perceived gender) of my partner. This is a very different experience of privilege than a fixed attribute such as skin color or a visible disability.

My intersectional identity includes being white, cisgendered, female, and queer. Both my cisgenderedness and whiteness give me a great deal of privilege. Although everyone's personal experience is their own and we are all unique, I realize that my representation and writing are filtered through my privilege and that my experience of LGBTQ+ oppression is quite different from that of an LGBTQ+ woman of color or a person who has more marginalized identities than I do. When I say that I am queer, I am indicating that I can be attracted to and partnered with all genders, including gender identities that don't have a binary male/female system. Some people use the word bisexual or pansexual for this identity. Bi-erasure and biphobia are very real experiences for many people like myself who don't fit neatly into a binary sexuality framework. I guarantee you that I am not confused or lying to myself because I "won't pick a side." There are far more than two sides. It is very difficult when people from both the straight and LGBTQ+ communities do not think that your identity "exists."

When partnered with a cisgendered male, things are pretty easy as far as what I have to deal with on outward appearance. Society seems to be respectful of me (not as a woman, but in a relationship context) when I adhere to the societal constructs that are currently in place. The pairing doesn't make people "uncomfortable." There are no worries about access to housing, employment, healthcare, or being in public spaces. There is freedom to hold hands without thinking about safety and that is just the tip of the iceberg on the unearned privileges handed to me. Multiply that by ten because of whiteness. I don't have to worry about my children being bullied because of my queerness either.

Being partnered with someone who is not a cisgendered male strips me of these privileges (although if I were partnered with a white transgender man and we "looked straight" I would still retain quite a few). I have the potential to make a lot of people uncomfortable. And do. Now society says that I am "different" at best, or horrific at worst. My relationships within my entire community change as a parent, professionally, and socially. In this pairing, we both have to work hard to stay safe. We can't travel to certain countries or even feel comfortable in some parts of our own country. We can't be mindless about public demonstrations of affection. We have to deal with staring all the time and potential weirdness for us at most every turn. Sometimes I am not sure if they are staring because they are not exposed to LGBTQ+ people very often and are curious, or if they are staring because they are homophobic, angry, and perhaps trying to intimidate us. There are microaggressions. Awkward silences. I have to prep my kids to the potential of bullying and rudeness about my identity. Sometimes it feels like so much more energy is expended to exist in public spaces in this partnership.

But I am thankful that I happen to live in one of the 21 states where I am protected against discrimination for housing, employment, and public accommodation. I am thankful that I live in a part of the country that is more diverse and queer friendly than others. I am thankful that there is community to be had within the field of music therapy. I am thankful that my kids have only known marriage equality and don't live within a religious community or oppressive environment that has fed them with hate speech. I am thankful that I can basically live an open and authentic life no matter who I am partnered with, even though my privilege can shift drastically.

I love the quote from Audre Lorde "If I didn't define myself for myself, I would be crunched into other people's fantasies for me and eaten alive" (1984, p.137). It resonates for me so deeply. She was a brilliant writer, civil rights activist, LGBTQ+ icon, womanist, feminist, and fierce black woman whose expressions about gender, sexuality, and race have always been incredibly powerful for me. I spent a LOT of years trying to define myself as to what I thought I "should" be or what seemed "right." At one point, I felt suffocated by the weight of living like that. It wasn't until I defined myself for myself and myself only that I was finally free.

Introduction

It is almost inevitable that every music therapy student or professional reading this book will work with someone who identifies as lesbian, gay, bisexual, transgender, queer or questioning, as well as additional identities indicated by the + sign including but not limited to non-binary, pansexual, asexual, intersex, and (LGBTQ+) no matter what region, age, population, or facility you work with/in. The American Music Therapy Association (AMTA) *Code of Ethics* states that we "provide quality client care regardless of the client's race, religion, age, sex, sexual orientation, gender identity or gender expression, ethnic or national origin, disability, health status, socio-economic status, marital status, or political affiliation" (1.1), and "identify and recognize their personal biases, avoiding discrimination in relationships with clients, colleagues, and others in all settings" (1.2) (AMTA, 2019).

Yet for many, familiarity about the LGBTQ+ community is lacking in education, training, and knowledge. Ahessy (2011) was the first to research, through universities and organizations, the shortage of global music therapy education and training specifically relating to LGB people. Ahessy (2011) also noted that the main education was focused on LGB people with HIV or AIDS. Thankfully, in recent years there has been an increased focus on LGBTQ+ education through the AMTA, and updated research on the current state of LGBTQ+ education and training on a global university and organizational level is warranted.

In a 2013 survey, Whitehead-Pleaux *et al.* found that 58 percent of music therapists had not received training regarding LGBTQ+ issues and from the ones who *had* received training, 59 percent did not feel prepared to work with people in the LGBTQ+ communities. Our attitudes about the LGBTQ+ community may include personal biases and/or misinformation. How do we as music therapists commit to becoming effective, supporting, and affirming music therapists to our LGBTQ+ community? What are possible theories that can inform our work? What are some music therapy models and accompanying interventions?

The LGBTQ+ experience

The LGBTQ+ experience and culture is broad and multifaceted and includes fashion, art, music, vernacular, social venues, media, and literature. The culture runs deeper than the iconic rainbow flag. It's nearly impossible to define the many subcultures and experiences of people who have a variety of marginalized identities related to gender or sexuality. The people within the LGBTQ+ umbrella are a mix of intersectional identities that include age, gender, class, ethnicity, race, culture, ability, and regional culture. Levels of power and privilege within each intersectional identity shift the person's experiences in and of the world. It's important to note that the variation of being "out" or "closeted" (or a mix of both depending on circumstances) also relates to privilege as well, and many factors, including safety.

LGBTQ+ people of color

The erasure of the voice and identity of people of color in the LGBTQ+ community is a prime example of disparities within a culture. White, affluent cisgendered males have historically been the mainstream identity most associated with the LGBTQ+ rights movement and what is "acceptable" in media portrayals. However, in 2012 it was estimated that one-third of the LGBTQ+ population are people of color and this includes large numbers of immigrants (Movement Advancement Project *et al.*, 2013). LGBTQ+ people of color face higher rates of unemployment and poverty for reasons including: educational barriers, taxation, hiring bias, discrimination in the workplace, and unequal pay (Movement Advancement Project *et al.*, 2013). At the time of writing this book, we are hopeful that the trend towards greater inclusivity and accurate representation of LGBTQ+ people of color continues. Nevertheless, this is an upward battle, as the systemic issues of racism, patriarchy, sexism, ableism, cisgenderism, and heteronormativity are rampant in 2019.

Violence against LGBTQ+ people

In 2018, the Federal Bureau of Investigation (FBI) reported that federal hate crimes in the United States had risen an alarming 17 percent, which continues a three-year upward trend and the largest increase in hate crimes since 9/11/01 (Fitzsimons, 2018). Fitzsimons also reports that 17 percent of the hate crimes have been targeted at people due to their gender identity or sexual orientation (2018). Sadly, Pezzella, Fetzer, and Keller (2019) insist that these numbers are still likely a major undercount of the total number of bias incidents, because a majority of hate crimes go unreported, as evidenced by the drastic difference in the FBI statistics and the National Crime Victimization Survey. In particular, transgender women of color are of higher risk, encompassing four out of five of all anti-transgender homicides due to anti-transgender stigma, racism, and sexism combined (Human Rights Campaign Foundation, 2018).

LGBTQ+ youth

Compared to growing up LGBTQ+ before 2010, there is currently a more supportive atmosphere and more support available depending on where you live in the country. That being said, a whopping 40 percent of homeless youth identify as LGBTQ+ (Human Rights Campaign Foundation, 2018). LGBTQ+ youth are twice as likely to be physically assaulted in some way, and 70 percent report being bullied at school (Human Rights Campaign, 2018). Additional stressors face LGBTQ+ youth of color due to bias around their intersecting identities, which further complicates the experience of being LGBTQ+ (Human Rights Campaign, 2018). Supportive environments and community, and free services to utilize in a crisis are essential to help mitigate the difficulties facing LGBTQ+ youth. In a meta-analysis of 62,923 participants, Marx and Kettrey (2016) found that the presence of a Gay Straight Alliance (GSA) within a school equates to significant decreases of self-reports of safety concerns, homophobic victimization, and remarks. The Trevor Project is a national service that offers free 24/7 intervention and suicide prevention services via text and phone to LGBTQ+ youth up to the age of 25 (The Trevor Project, 2019a). Its research has shown that "youth with at least one accepting adult were significantly less likely to report a suicide attempt" in relation to disclosing their LGBTQ+ status (The Trevor Project, 2019b).

Current legal issues of LGBTQ+ people

It appears that there is false sense of security regarding the legal protections of LGBTQ+ people following the 2015 ruling by the Supreme Court declaring same-sex marriages legal in all states. At the time of this writing, *30 states* have laws in place that could deny an LGBTQ+ person housing and services, and do not protect them from being fired for their identity. Only 15 states have laws that prohibit discrimination against students in public education on the basis of sexual orientation or gender identity. Only 16 states have laws banning the use of conversion therapy with youth by licensed professionals (Human Rights Campaign, 2019). While the movement towards equality is hopeful progress for LGBTQ+ people, we are a long way from actual equality and safety on a legal level.

LGBTQ+ affirming music therapy

The above information is provided to help inform you of various issues that may cause stress for your LGBTQ+ clients or their families and community. When working with LGBTQ+ clients, do not pathologize being LGBTQ+ as the problem, but instead consider all of the minority stress processes which impact their experience in music therapy. It is critically important to not assume that the presenting issue is related to being LGBTQ+ or to make their sexual orientation and/or gender identity the focus of your work.

There are several resources available within music therapy literature to assist in further education about LGBTQ+ topics and affirming practices, including in-depth definitions of common terms, the use of pronouns, appropriate language, creating inclusive assessments, forms, and documentation (Whitehead-Pleaux et al., 2012; Oswanski et al., 2018), historical realities versus popular myths (Hardy & Whitehead-Pleaux, 2017), resources for educators (York, 2015), resources for supervision (Oswanski et al., 2019), and general resources including online training, LGBTQ+ civil rights and legal organizations, and media (Hardy & Whitehead-Pleaux, 2017; Oswanski et al., 2018; Oswanski et al., 2019). It is *imperative* to seek education beyond this chapter in order to provide quality affirmative care for LGBTQ+ people.

The focus of this chapter is on identifying theoretical domains that can provide an open and affirming LGBTQ+ practice by viewing the client within the lens of interrelated factors instead of individual isolation within their presenting issue. Although there are many differences within the LGBTQ+ community, the "shared experience of living outside dominant sexuality and sex/gender norms, and the close links between sexuality and sex/gender, merit an inclusive approach" (Clarke *et al.*, 2010, p.5).

We feel that the safest and most effective music therapy practices for LGBTQ+ people are intersectional, non-heterosexist, non-genderist, and radically inclusive approaches to therapy—not based in pathology. Although there can be significant crossover in many of the areas of practice we are listing—queer, community, social justice, and feminist—their theoretical foundations shape how they view the presenting issue of the client differently from each other. Generally, the orientations listed above take a macro systems view of the client's current needs and presenting issues. By accounting for the myriad of interrelated and interdependent influences when working with a client, the therapist has a greater awareness of how the intersectional identity impacts the therapeutic process. Queer, social justice, and feminist foundations consider the impact of multiple influences, including marginalization and privilege, on the person. Community music therapy is context-based and can *create community* as well as *create awareness of/for a community*. Many music therapists practice with a blend of these orientations in order to provide comprehensive care for their clients and their communities.

Queer theory and queer music therapy

If you search the phrase "what is queer theory" you will get a result of thousands of articles and books on the topic: queer theory related to gender and sexuality, queer theory related to physical education pedagogy, queer theory implemented in public relations, queer theory as it relates to ethnicity, race, culture, and beyond. Queer theory is a multifaceted and complex topic. Some queer theorists even feel that offering a definition is conforming to societal norms and, in itself, is counter to the principles of queer theory (Sullivan, 2003). When in the context of LGBTQ+ therapy, queer theory can be very broadly defined as a way of challenging the notion of fixed sexual identities or a fixed gender binary (Jagose, 1996), which have been created by heteronormative and cisnormative societal constructs.

In 2016, Bain, Grzanka, and Crowe delineated the connection between queer theory and music therapy and suggested a move towards a radically inclusive approach to music therapy (queer music therapy) with LGBTQ+ people. Queer music therapy would offer an opportunity to combat heteronormativity though highlighting the complex nature of sexuality, positively influence interpersonal relationships, empower queer people to express and live their sexual and gender identity, support of expression surrounding conflicts due to oppression, highlight the commonality of cause vs. identity, and counteract negative social pressures (Bain *et al.*, 2016).

In 2017, Boggan, Grzanka, and Bain implemented qualitative research to critically evaluate the queer music therapy model above. Twelve board-certified music therapists were interviewed who identified as LGBTQ+ or worked with LGBTQ+ clients. Questions included music therapy background, experiences with LGBTQ+ clients, and feedback on the Bain *et al.* (2016) model. The data was analyzed using a critical discourse approach, and indicated that the queer music therapy model has strengths, including the rejection of pathologizing LGBTQ+ identities, a community music therapy focus, and an emphasis less on commonalities and more on a common cause. However, the exploration highlighted needed development in areas of intersectional queer identity in relation to age and ability status. Other themes unearthed were the lack of diversity in the field, privilege and barriers in the current educational programs, as well as the clear lack of multicultural awareness training in our undergraduate programs (Boggan *et al.*, 2017).

Social justice music therapy

Social justice movements have a long history of the use of music as motivating, connecting, and empowering people. In the literature of the last 20 years, music therapy concepts point to the hypothesis of music as an influence towards socio-political transformation (Baines, 2013; Hadley, 2006; Kenny, 2006; Stige, 2002; Vaillancourt, 2012). Although it is difficult to arrive at one concise definition of social justice, it can broadly be defined as the fair and equitable distribution of privilege, opportunities and wealth in society (Social justice, 2019).

In some community and feminist music therapy contexts, social justice is an integral part of direct practice (Ansdell, 2002; Baines, 2013; Curtis, 2015; Hadley, 2006; Ruud, n.d.; Vaillancourt, 2012). Baines (2013) suggests in order to "do" anti-oppressive music therapy, we have to "continue to seek to address social inequities on multiple levels including through regular social action" (p.4). We feel that social justice ally education and development should be a mandated requirement for all music therapists to provide a framework for affirming, anti-oppressive therapy with marginalized individuals, groups, and communities. Referring to social justice ally development, Oswanski and Donnenwerth (2017) state that the "development and practice of an ally is not optional as a music therapist, but an ethical requirement" (p.259). While many music therapy students and professionals are interested in social justice activism and ally development, they are uncertain how to integrate these concepts into their clinical work.

In order to practice social justice music therapy, one must undergo training, education and critical reflection on social justice issues. Curtis (2012) points out that there are many different ways to approach social justice work, just as there are many different ways to approach music therapy practice. That being said, the foundation of social justice ally development and direct practice *must* include the music therapist engaging in ongoing critical self-reflection regarding their awareness of their identity markers, values, and privileges (Oswanski & Donnenwerth, 2017). As Vaillancourt (2012) points out, social and cultural countertransference is a concern without examination of the music therapist's socio-cultural experiences. In work with LGBTQ+ people, this process is paramount considering the heteronormative and cisgendered society that filters our socio-cultural experiences. In-depth personal analysis of organized religious beliefs should also be included. Something important to note from the counseling literature is that "counselors' higher frequency of church attendance, political conservatism, heterosexist, and rigid and authoritarian orientations of religious identity exhibit more negative attitudes and prejudice towards LGBTQ+ people" (Balkin, Schlosser & Levi, 2009; Bidell, 2014; Farmer, 2017; Oswanski *et al.*, 2019; Rainey & Trusty, 2007; Sanabria, 2012; Satcher & Schumacker, 2009).

Service learning projects, conference presentations, continuing education courses, community education, and online resources through social justice organizations are mechanisms for obtaining further education. An excellent peer-reviewed interdisciplinary journal for social justice, inclusivity, and socio-cultural awareness in music therapy is *Voices*.[1]

After training and critical self-reflection, direct action is the next step. Without action, social justice music therapy is not being practiced. National organizations to partner with for LGBTQ+ social justice advocacy and action include, but are not limited to, the Human Rights Campaign, the National Center for Lesbian Rights, the Transgender Law Program, and the American Civil Liberties Union. There are many ways to advocate for and with the LGBTQ+ community, including working to change discriminatory laws and organizational policies, working with local organizations and communities, working towards decreasing LGBTQ+ healthcare disparities, political action, or getting involved in grassroots LGBTQ+ advocacy.

Community music therapy and health musicking

Community music therapy and health musicking are intrinsically connected by addressing the health of both a person and the health of their community. Musicking, which means *to music*, is a term credited to Chris Small, who describes the act of taking part in music, be it dancing, listening, performing, practicing, composing (Small, 1998). As Bonde (2011) and Small (1998) point out, musicking is a relational experience, as a person will establish a relationship with the music they are accessing.

The topic of community music therapy is broad and the definitions vary depending on the music therapist and their approach. In 2002, Stige stated that two main notions of community music therapy

---

1   https://voices.no/index.php/voices/index

exist: 1) music therapy in a community context, and 2) music therapy for change in a community. Both notions require that the therapist be sensitive to social and cultural contexts, but the latter notion to a more radical degree departs from conventional modern notions of therapy in that goals and interventions relate directly to the community in question. Music therapy, then, may be considered cultural and social engagement and may function as community action; the community is not only a context for work but also a context to be worked with (p.328).

As highlighted earlier in this chapter, in order to provide affirming and anti-oppressive music therapy services for LGBTQ+ people we need to move away from the conventional modern notions of therapy and towards radically inclusive and empowering therapeutic constructs to appropriately serve our clients. Ruud (n.d.) articulates: "People become ill, sometimes not because of physical processes, but because they become disempowered by ignorance and lack of social understanding" (p.4). Daily microaggressions, marginalized identity stressors, discrimination, isolation, fear of violence, and lack of basic protections through oppressive laws place LGBTQ+ people at high risk for "illness(es)" related to their spiritual, physical, and emotional health. Community music therapy through health musicking can offer a platform for individual and collective community goals to be achieved simultaneously that ultimately create change and increase the quality of health for LGBTQ+ people.

Bonde (2011) points out that *health musicking* can be a professional music therapy practice, community musicking, and also lay-therapeutic musicking (meaning it is not facilitated by a professional and can be solitary). Often clients are looking for health through music outside a professional one-on-one music therapy session. Encouraging participation in community musicking and supporting the development of lay-therapeutic musicking can also be a comprehensive approach for LGBTQ+ clients towards health and wellness. In direct practice, community music therapy in this context might involve creating a band or orchestra at a community LGBTQ+ space, facilitating a choir for trans and/or non-binary singers, or the creation of an opera or musical theater piece written by the LGBTQ+ community. All of these examples can eventually lead to performances, or further expansion to support and empower the LGBTQ+ community. Queer music therapy support groups using improvisation, songwriting, relaxation techniques, dance, movement, and health musicking that push against the constraints of societal norms and allow a safe space for expression are also powerful forms of community music therapy.

Feminist music therapy

Feminist music therapy, which can be practiced with any gender (Curtis, 2012), has been described by Hahna and Schwantes (2011) as a philosophical approach with numerous perspectives in music therapy practice and education. Curtis (2012) asserts that feminist music therapy incorporates community music therapy with the addition of feminist analysis, including gender and power as the central tenants. Considering how much gender and power play a role in the repression of LGBTQ+ people, a feminist analysis offers another layer of strength in implementing inclusive music therapy practice. Feminist music therapy examines the intersectional dimensions of clients. As Seabrook (2019) explains:

> Intersectionality is a specific feminist theory that interrogates both the ways that different identities combine to create unique and complex dynamics of oppression and power for individuals and communities as well as the broader social structures that sustain the marginalization of certain identity positions. (p.2)

Because of the focus on the layered marginalized identities of LGBTQ+ people, a feminist music therapy lens can be an incredibly affirming and empowering approach to music therapy practice. Hadley (2006) and Curtis (2013, 2017) have indicated that if we are to provide a gender and culturally sensitive practice as music therapists, it is wise to obtain further education on feminist music therapy practices.

Clinical interventions

There has been little research published in music therapy literature

on work with LGBTQ+ people. Due to shifting trends we are hopeful
that young music therapy clinicians will be adding to this body of
knowledge in the coming years, as we have seen a sharp increase in
presentations on LGBTQ+ issues since 2012 when the Whitehead-
Pleaux and colleagues *Best Practices* document was published.

Bain, Grzanka, and Crowe (2016) highlight several therapeutic
interventions based in queer music therapy with LGBTQ+ youth.
Some of these interventions include *music autobiographical
assessment* to help "gain a holistic picture of a client's need in
music therapy" (Bain *et al.*, 2016, p.27). During this intervention,
one creates a past, present, and future timeline of their life using
song choices that resonate or connect to important life events
and how one identifies with them. This intervention can be used
in many different forms, to explore gender, sexual identity, and
identify oppression and discrimination. Bain *et al.* (2016) explains,
"*queering* this intervention can provide focus on empowerment,
affirmation rather than reinforce heteronormativity" (p.27). *Gender
bender song parodies and performance* can allow for exploration and
affirmation of gender and sexuality. Gender bending is the act of
transforming, bending, and/or defining traditional, stereotypical,
or expected gender roles and gender expression. Mainstream
music is predominantly heteronormative and gendered. This can
feel oppressive if one's gender or sexual orientation is not often
represented in the music one hears. Gender bending these songs,
either by filling in the blank songwriting or performing from
a different gender can *queer* the experience. Choosing to play
with gender, gender roles, and sexuality during song parodies or
performance can challenge the pervasive heteronormative narrative
and create the space for liberating and affirming music therapy.
Critical lyric analysis, discussion, and engagement around the lyrics
of a song can be particularly powerful when using a song that has a
queer narrative or point of view.

Hardy (2018) conducted a mixed-methods pilot study to
investigate the influence of a community-based music therapy
workshop with transgender adolescents. The researcher created a
one-day community-based workshop that consisted of:

- non-referential and referential group improvisation— including focused improvisations on issues related to the LGBTQ+ experience, such as directives to play how gender dysphoria feels, and non-referential improvisations based off of a chord progression

- queering the dance space—allowing freedom to move outside the limiting societal binary gender roles and rules. This can be empowering and affirming

- group songwriting—creating cohesion, reducing feelings of isolation, creating opportunities for one to creatively express oneself, celebrating differences, commonalities, strengths, and resilience. In this approach to songwriting, the piece of music can also become a ritualized anthem that can be utilized for opening or closing a session.

Results included meaningful changes in the areas of perception of gender identity, increased confidence, a decrease in gender identity questioning, a rise in self-esteem, and an increased sense of community, with the biggest impact in an increase in positive coping (Hardy, 2018).

In their 2019 master's thesis, Gumble weaves in queer theory as a piece of an autoethnographic framework that explores the possibilities of gender-affirming voicework in music therapy. Voicework with transgender or non-binary clients can include changes to one's voice to better align with one's gender and is traditionally provided by speech and language pathologists. The American Speech-Language-Hearing Association lists the voice and communication services provided for transgender and gender-diverse populations, including assessment and treatment goals which can target the following areas: vocal health, resonance, pitch, intonation, volume, articulation, language, and non-verbal communication (American Speech-Language-Hearing Association, 2019).

In music therapy, voice feminization, masculinization or gender-neutralizing goals can be addressed and explored as well. This might include support in speech and vocal changes, singing range, and non-verbal communication. Clients might also seek music therapy to provide an outlet for creative expression and emotional support while experiencing and working on vocal changes. Achieving a voice that is congruent with one's true gender can decrease gender dysphoria, as well as provide a critical piece to one's quality of life, emotional health, and physical safety. While the music therapist may have a unique skillset to assess and work on transgender and non-binary voicework, there is a specific training and education that needs to occur as well as possible co-treatment with the client's speech therapist or other related disciplines. Three resources available for educating oneself in voicework with transgender clients are: *Voice and Communication Therapy for the Transgender/Gender Diverse Client* (Adler, Hirsch, & Pickering, 2019), *The Voice Book for Trans and Non-Binary People* (Mills & Stoneham, 2017), and *The Singing Teacher's Guide to Transgender Voices* (Jackson & Kremer, 2018).

When preparing music therapy interventions with LGBTQ+ clients, whether using improvisation, lyric analysis, voicework, music and art experientials, songwriting or any form of musicking, it is important to have a frame of reference for the musical history and culture of the LGBTQ+ community. Like most marginalized groups, there are historical connections that have impacted the history of LGBTQ+ musical culture. The following section provides a short overview of LGBTQ+ music in the United States from the 1920s through to 2019.

LGBTQ+ artists and music through the decades

Every letter in the LGBTQ+ acronym has its own unique musical culture and history, from the lesbian singer songwriters of the 1970s to the gay men's dance club scene of the 1980s, to the representation of LGBTQ+ artists in the current hip-hop scene. As within most cultures, and arguably even more so within the LGBTQ+ umbrella, there is variety and difference within the many subcultures. LGBTQ+ music and artists cover all styles of music, including classical, jazz, country, pop, disco, techno, folk, funk, musical theater, camp, rock, punk, metal, hip-hop, rap, and so on.

In the book, *Cultural Intersections in Music Therapy*, Hardy and Whitehead-Pleaux (2017) provide details about the meaning of

LGBTQ+ music, roles, performers, venues, and songs. Within their chapter, they discuss how music can create and unite the LGBTQ+ community. Adding a historical perspective to this discussion, we can thread together a timeline addressing the significance of highlighted songs, musicians, and performers of the LGBTQ+ community with the current events of the times.

Music therapists may provide care for LGBTQ+ clients of all ages. The use of music that is connected to the client's culture and identity can be a very effective and affirming tool. It's important to have a strong understanding of the music and also the interwoven historical context of the client's generational LGBTQ+ cultural experience to provide accurate music therapy services.

1920–1930s

Prohibition began in 1920 and ran until 1933, which resulted in the prominence of speakeasies. The Pansy Craze is the term used to describe the gay music and entertainment club scene at that time, which was part of the speakeasy scene (Elledge, 2010). There were fewer discriminatory laws on the books that specifically singled out LGBTQ+ people than in the following decades. Although being LGBTQ+ was not the norm and there was still plenty of ignorance and discrimination in America regarding LGBTQ+ people, there was also more tolerance and acceptance in the entertainment industry, particularly in urban areas. Many musicians could be more open about their sexuality and gender expression within their music and performance, and some made their expression of gender and sexuality part of their act.

Within the Pansy Craze era, many performers performed in drag and there were songs with double entendre and tongue-in-cheek lyrical content hinting at homosexuality and gender bending. Popular drag performers included Jean Malin and Gladys Bentley. This is considered to be the beginning of the gay nightlife scene, including drag and camp, music and dancing. There was also a blues scene that included sex positive and queer sexualities within their lyrics and performers. Bessie Jackson's (also known as Lucille Bogan) "BD Women's Blues" (Bogan, 1935) and Ma Rainey's "Prove it On Me Blues" (Rainey, 1928) both openly express queer sexuality and were written and sung by queer performers. BD is short for "Bull Dagger," a term used for a butch lesbian at that time.

1940s–early 1960s

During and after World War II, there was a strong push towards social conservatism in America. Federal and local laws were passed allowing for discrimination against LGBTQ+ people, including a ban on holding federal jobs. In 1952, the first edition of the *Diagnostic and Statistical Manual (DSM-I)*, published by the American Psychiatric Association, classified being "homosexual" as being a mental disorder and as a "sociopathic personality disturbance" (Drescher, 2015), which gives an indication of the intense climate of hostility towards LGBTQ+ people at that time. In the entertainment industry, the Hays Code, sometimes known as the Moral Production Code, banned LGBTQ+ representation in film and theater and attempted to "bind movies to Judeo-Christian morality," including suppressing films with themes of birth control, drinking, suicide, criminal violence, sexual license, abortion, race relations and the depiction of national or ethnic groups (Vaughn, 1990, pp.39–40).

By the middle of the 1950s, an opposition against increasing gender and race discrimination had begun with the civil rights and feminist movements. There was also the development of Daughters of Bilitis (DOB), the first known lesbian rights organization in the United States. The DOB hosted small, safer private social functions, trying to avoid police raids and the threats of violence and discrimination in bars and clubs (Gallo, 2006).

During this time period, LGBTQ+ musicians and performers were in or returning to the closet. It was a dangerous time to be out about sexuality or gender that did not conform to heterosexual, binary cisgender roles, which is reflected in the music. Many LGBTQ+ musicians were not out publicly, such as: Dusty Springfield, Little Richard, Leslie Gore, Billie Holiday and Leonard Bernstein. Billy Strayhorn was one of the few musicians and composers who was out with their sexuality. Jackie Shane, a pioneer transgender rhythm and blues (R&B) and soul vocalist, was not officially "out" in the 1960s but refused an offer to appear on *The Ed Sullivan Show* when they made the offer contingent on her presenting as male (Farber, 2019).

Despite constant police raids and threats of violence, there were still some gay clubs that included drag and camp shows. The Jewel Box Revue was one of these clubs and one of their famous singers and performers was Stormé DeLarverie (Yardley, 2014). The Jewel Box Revue was a variety show in which Stormé dressed as a man and the rest of the cast, all men, dressed as women (Yardley, 2014).

Late 1960s–1970s

By the end of the 1960s the LGBTQ+ community had become more organized and began to fight back against police violence, threats and bar raids against them. This was happening all over the country, but one of the most powerful events was the Stonewall Riot of 1969. This is considered to be the beginning of the LGBTQ+ rights movement. (History.com, 2017). As the LGBTQ+ rights movement continued to grow and become organized, we saw the first gay pride marches, and the inception of gay/lesbian band and choruses, some of which still exist today, such as the Gay Men's Chorus.

During the late 1960s and 1970s, the mainstream American culture began to shift again toward a more open, sex-positive attitude about sexuality led by the youth and hippy movement. This is the time that LGBTQ+ music and the club scene developed more fully. In the rock genre, disco and glam rock become popular music for dancing and dance clubs. Both have elements of freedom of gender expression and freedom of sexuality. Some of the LGBTQ+ artists and bands performing at this time included David Bowie, Freddie Mercury, Sylvester, Elton John, and The Village People.

There was also a women's feminist folk and singer songwriter movement in America during this time. The music had folk roots and included vocals, and accompaniment of acoustic guitar or piano and fewer electric instruments. The movement had a strong lesbian presence in both musicians and audiences. The women's music festivals were created to give women musicians a place to perform and have their music recognized as well as to provide a safe place for women to celebrate and enjoy this music and each other. At its height, there were over 20 states that had some form of annual women's music festival, and some continued for decades after this. One of the largest and longest-running festivals was the Michigan's Womyn's Music Festival. Some of the artists from this movement include Holly Near, Meg Christian, Cris Williamson, and Joan Armatrading.

A few important LGBTQ+ songs from this time period include:

- "You Make Me Feel (Mighty Real)," performed by Sylvester (Wirrick & Sylvester, 1978)

- "YMCA," performed by The Village People (Morali & Willis, 1978)

- "Boys Keep Swinging," performed by David Bowie (Eno & Bowie, 1979)

- "Dancing Queen," performed by ABBA, (Andersson, Ulvaeus, & Anderson, 1976)

- "We Are Family," performed by Sister Sledge (Edwards & Rodgers, 1979)

- "Got To Be Real," performed by Cheryl Lynn (Lynn, Paich, & Foster, 1978)

- "I Will Survive," performed by Gloria Gaynor (Perren & Fekaris, 1978).

1980s–early 1990s

The most impactful circumstance of the 1980s for LGBTQ+ culture, by far was the HIV/AIDS crisis. By the end of the decade, there were "At least 100,000 reported cases of AIDS in the United States and [an] estimated 400,000 cases worldwide" (History.com, 2017). In the LGBTQ+ community, especially for gay men, people were losing their entire community within a decade. Radical social justice LGBTQ+ organizations such as ACT UP and Queer Nation were created to fight against discrimination and demand visibility, protections, and medical funding (Morris, n.d.). LGBTQ+ performers like Freddie

Mercury's and Sylvester's AIDS-related deaths, and the impact of AIDS affected the entire music industry. Musicians who were out in the 1970s were pressured to go back into the closet during the 1780s and 1990s.

During the 1980s and early 1990s, music videos and *MTV* became a new influence for popular music, adding a visual element. Musical artists wore flashy, colorful clothing or leather. There was a playfulness to gender expression with make-up and dance moves that were connected to LGBTQ+ culture, while still very few of the artists were publically out about their sexuality, at least within the entertainment industry. An example of this dichotomy is George Michael of Wham, Pete Burns of Dead or Alive, and Rob Halford of Judas Priest. A rare few musicians did come out publicly in the late 1980s, including Elton John and Boy George.

There were also number of British male groups who were composed largely of gay men, including Soft Cell, Frankie Goes to Hollywood, Erasure, Pet Shop Boys and Depeche Mode. RuPaul is an LGBTQ+ superstar who came onto the scene during the 1990s. Joan Jett, Melissa Etheridge, K.D. Lang, Debbie Harry, the Indigo Girls, Tracy Chapman, and Ani DiFranco were important musicians of the LGBTQ+ women's music scene of the 1980s and 1990s.

A few important LGBTQ+ songs from this time period include:

- "I'm Coming Out," performed by Diana Ross (Edwards & Rodgers, 1980)

- "I Want to Break Free," performed by Queen (Deacon, 1984)

- "A Little Respect," performed by Erasure (Clarke & Bell, 1988)

- "Vogue," performed by Madonna (Madonna & Pettibone, 1989)

- "Freedom! '90," performed by George Michael (Michael, 1989)

- "Groove Is in the Heart," performed by Deee-Lite (Brill *et al.*, 1990)

- "Come To My Window," performed by Melissa Etheridge (Etheridge, 1993)

- "Supermodel," performed by RuPaul (RuPaul, Harry, & Tee, 1992)

- "If I Could Turn Back Time," performed by Cher (Warren, 1989)

- "Closer to Fine," performed by the Indigo Girls (Saliers, 1988)

- "Constant Craving," performed by K.D. Lang (Lang & Mink, 1991)

- "True Colors," performed by Cyndi Lauper (Kelly & Steinberg, 1986).

Mid 1990s–2010

The post-AIDS crisis climate of the 1990s continued to be a harsh environment for the LGBTQ+ community. This time period produced many anti-gay policies like Don't Ask, Don't Tell policies, which at the time was actually an improvement for LGBTQ+ military members being dishonorably discharged from the military, yet it still created an anti-LGBTQ+ atmosphere. President Clinton, making it legal for states to refuse to recognize same-sex marriages, signed the Defense of Marriage Act (DOMA) into law.

However, the 1990s were also a creative time for female musicians who were gaining success in the male-dominated music industry. A good number of these musicians identified as bisexual or lesbian. With ties to the women's music festivals of the 1970s and 1980s, the Lilith Fair was created by Sarah McLachlan. It was a musical tour consisting of women and women-led bands in the late 1990s. Some of the LGBTQ+ identified women who performed at the Lilith Fair were: Indigo Girls, Tegan and Sara, Tracy Chapman, Brandi Carlile, Queen Latifah, and Miranda Lambert. The 1990s also saw a rise in Riot Girl music, with roots in feminism and punk music. This style of feminist punk music started off in the Pacific Northwest. LGBTQ+ musicians and bands in Riot Girl scene where also known as Queer Core and included Sleater-Kinny, Team Dresch, Tribe 8, and Bikini Kill to name a few. There were also gay male queer core bands, including Pansy Division.

A few important LGBTQ+ songs from this time period include:

- "32 Flavors," performed by Ani Difranco (DiFranco, 1995)

- "Heavy Cross," performed by Gossip (Ditto, Paine, & Billie, 2009)

- "The Origin of Love," from the musical *Hedwig and the Angry Inch* (Trask & Mitchell, 1999)

- "Rebel Girl," performed by Bikini Kill (Hanna *et al.*, 1993).

2010s through current

Since 2010, we have seen great strides toward LGBTQ+ equality, protection, and rights gained, including Marriage Equality in 2015 and Don't Ask, Don't Tell repealed in 2011. In particular, transgender rights have gained national support for protections. However, from 2017 to the present day we have seen some of these rights taken away, including a transgender ban in the military. It is our hope that as we look forward and past the 2020s, we will continue the progress made and see LGBTQ+ equalities and protections achieved and championed.

Current transgender and non-binary musicians from 2010 onwards include Laura Jane Grace from Against Me, Anhoni, Mx. Justin Vivian Bond, Shea Diamond, Big Freedia, and Lucas Silveria. Other LGBTQ+ musicians from this time period include Janelle Monáe, Sam Smith, Sia, King Princess, Hayley Kiyoko, and Mykki Blanco. There are and will be many, many more to come.

A few important LGBTQ+ songs from this time period include:

- "True Trans Soul Rebel," performed by Against Me! (Grace, 2013)

- "Born This Way," performed by Lady Gaga (Germanotta & Laursen, 2010)

- "She Keeps Me Warm," performed by Mary Lambert (Lambert, 2013)

- "Closer," performed by Tegan and Sara (Quin, Quin, & Kurstin, 2012)

- "Raise You Up," from the musical *Kinky Boots* (Lauper, 2013)

- "I Am Her," performed by Shea Diamond (Diamond, 2018)

- "Make Me Feel," performed by Janelle Monáe (Robinson *et al.*, 2018).

CLINICAL CASE SCENARIOS

The following are clinical case scenarios to stimulate conversation and learning about working with LGBTQ+ people in music therapy. Consider the complexities of each case, including personal bias, heteronormativity, intersectionality, and LGBTQ+ misinformation.

CASE SCENARIO 1

You are a music therapist at an adult intensive outpatient mental health hospital facility. As you are attending the weekly team treatment meeting, the team brings up a patient who is a transgender woman. You listen to a team member make rude comments about this patient's gender expression and not respect her pronouns.

In your initial music therapy intake meeting with this patient, she had requested she/her/hers pronouns, and asked to be called a name that did not match the name on her facility intake form. You had noticed that this patient was expressing both masculine and feminine features in their presentation. They were wearing a feminine dress and heels. However, the dress was small and poor fitting. They wore make up that appeared very bold. They also had body hair, a beard coming in and short masculine hair.

A nurse at the team meeting referred to this young woman as a "hot mess" and continued to refer to her as "he." The nurse commented, "If he wants to be taken seriously, he should clean up his appearance and make a better effort to look more female." Several people at the meeting snickered and agreed.

Study questions

1. How do you best advocate for this patient in regard to her gender, pronouns and gender expression? How do you address the team members who have made these remarks?

2. Why might a patient's name and gender not match what is on their intake form, driver's license or other forms of identification?

3. What should your music therapy intake form include to make sure you are aware of patients' gender and pronouns? Most inclusive option for gender/sex would be a blank space to fill in. If it needs to be boxes to check, make sure the form has options for transgender male, transgender female, intersex, gender non-binary, and other, as well as male and female options. Make sure your intake form has an area for pronouns. Again, most inclusive would be a blank space to fill in. If there are boxes to check, include they/them/their as well as others along with she/her/hers and he/him/his options.)

4. What resources might you use to help support your advocacy for this patient? (Are there enforced non-discrimination policies that specifically protect LGBTQ people and gender identity at your facility? What does it say about gender and gender expression? Are there gender expression and/or transgender non-discrimination laws in place for your city? State?)

5. How might class, race and gender have an impact on this situation?

   i. How could privilege or the lack thereof impact what medical care is given and ability to receive transitioning medical procedures and treatment for this client?

   ii. How might a trans woman of color be seen differently from a white trans man in our society?

   iii. What might be the root of this difference?

6. Do this patient's mental health issues impact the way others process her gender? How?

7. How does one's views of gender being either a binary system or a gender spectrum impact how we see this patient's gender and gender expression as healthy or unhealthy?

8. How might you affirm and support this patient's gender and identify through music therapy?

CASE SCENARIO 2

You are a music therapist working at a residential senior center. On your caseload is an elderly male client who is quiet, mostly stays in his room and keeps to himself. You have recently learned that this man identifies as gay, and his long-time partner has just died. They had been together since the 1970s, and this client is now showing signs of grief and depression. This is new information for you because his intake form had written that he was not married, and you had always assumed that he was single and heterosexual.

Study questions

1. Does this new information change your perception of this client?

2. What is heteronormativity? How can this have a negative impact on our relationship and treatment of clients? How might it impact our understanding of one's life experiences, identity and family?

3. Why might someone in a residential senior center be in the closet about their sexuality?

   i. Within older generations, what are some of the shared life experiences being LGBTQ in the 1960s, 1950s, 1940s and earlier that are different from today's LGBTQ youth? And how might that impact their sense of safety to disclose their sexuality and identity?

4. What can you do to acknowledge this new information in your next music therapy session together?

5. What questions can you ask to learn more about this gentleman's life history, his life as a gay man, and his relationship with his partner?

6. How can you acknowledge and address this person's grief at losing his long-term partner musically?

7. What musical artists and songs might you use that are in this client's demographic which now you know includes identifying as LGBTQ+?

CASE SCENARIO 3

You are a music therapist in an adolescent brain injury rehabilitation center. You are meeting a client for the first time in a music therapy group. You have not had a chance to see the client's intake form and are unaware of the client's gender or pronouns. Halfway through the group, you refer to the client using she/her/hers pronouns. The client corrects you and informs you that they go by they/them/theirs pronouns.

Study questions

1. What is a respectful way to address misgendering someone? (Answer: What should you do: Apologize, correct yourself and move on. Be conscious of using the correct pronouns moving forward. What should you avoid doing: Avoid long-winded explanations and apologies. This can be embarrassing for the misgendered person and also moves the focus from the person who deserves the apology and onto you and your discomfort.)

2. What might you do when running future groups to help prevent this situation from occurring again? (Answer: 1) Have intake forms that ask for pronouns. The most inclusive being a space to fill in the blank. If using boxes to check, make sure there

are "they/them/theirs" and also "other" as options along with "she/her/hers" and "he/him/his." (Answer: 2) Include pronouns as part of introductions at the beginning of your session. Begin with yourself "Hi my name is…, my pronouns are she/her. Can we all go around the room introducing ourselves and include pronouns as well?" (Answer: 3) In general, don't assume gender. Use gender-neutral language when addressing group members, such as, "They chose a song to share" versus "She chose a song to share."

3. What does it mean to have they/them pronouns?

    i. Classroom exercise: Practice how to use they/them in singular form in a conversation. In pairs, take five minutes to discuss something you did recently with a date or friend. For example, discuss going out to dinner or going to a concert or a coffee date; however, use only gender-neutral pronouns when talking. Have the class list neural pronoun options: they/them/theirs, person, folks, everyone, ya'll, and so on.

4. What does it mean to identify as gender non-binary, gender queer, gender fluid, agender?

    i. What is the gender spectrum and how does it differ from the binary lens of gender?

    ii. There are many terms that fall under a non-binary umbrella. How many gender identities and definitions do you know?

5. How might this information change how you perceive this client?

6. What might you do to exhibit support and a safe space for non-binary clients in your group?

    i. How might you be more inclusive clinically and musically to your non-binary clients?

CASE SCENARIO 4

You are a music therapist in a residential treatment facility that focuses on substance abuse and eating disorders. During an individual session with a young woman, she makes a comment about another patient, "I don't want to sit next to her, she's a nasty dyke. You know what I mean? I've got to watch my back with her."

Study questions

1. How do you address this? In the moment? In follow-up? (Answer: The Gay, Lesbian & Straight Education Network's *Safe Space Kit. A Guide to Supporting Lesbian, Gay, Bisexual and Transgender Students in Your School* has a section titled "Respond to Anti-LGBT Language and Behavior" (p.16) that is useful when discussing this topic. While it is meant as a tool for teachers, much of the information can also be used by music therapists.)

2. Would you address homophobic language in an individual session differently from a group session? How and why? What are some possible responses to LGBTQ+- derogatory comments?

   i. Classroom exercise: create a list of possible responses to homophobic and derogatory remarks both in an individual session and a group setting.

3. If you replaced the word "dyke" with a racial slur, would you address the comments differently? How and why?

4. Would you react differently if the patient stated, "Yeah, I'll sit next to her. She's alright. She's a dyke, you know what I mean?"

   i. Is the word "dyke" always a derogatory word? If not, when is it not?

5. What is reclaimed language? How is it used in the LGBTQ+ community? Who can use it? What can you do to support the patient at whom the comment was aimed?

6. What impact can homophobic and LGBTQ+- derogatory

language have on your LGBTQ+ clients? What about the impact beyond LGBTQ+- identified clients?

CASE SCENARIO 5

You are a music therapist in a children's hospital. A 6-year-old child has just been admitted and while reading the intake form you see that this child has two moms. You are preparing your first session with this child and will be meeting the child's parents in this session as well.

Study questions

1. When prepping for your first sessions with this child, what might you do or say to indicate you are an LGBTQ+ ally? How might you exhibit support and validation to this child and parents during your session with them?

2. What might you do musically to validate this child's family unit and experience?

3. Can you think of ways this family might experience stress and discomfort from heteronormativity and/or microaggressions in a hospital setting?

CASE SCENARIO 6

You are a music therapist in private practice. One of your clients is black and identifies as bisexual. She is coming to music therapy to address generalized anxiety and depression, and to develop coping skills. She has expressed to you that she has constant feelings of isolation and invisibility regarding her sexuality and her identity. She expresses feeling unaccepted in the straight and gay world. She has heard messages from the straight community and gay community such as, "Nobody is bisexual, you're just a closeted gay," "Bisexuals just can't make up their mind," "Bisexuals want it all," and "Bisexuals cannot be in monogamous relationships." She also expresses how some of her straight black friends perceive being LGBTQ+ as a white thing, stating "We don't do that."

Study questions

1. What stressors and microaggressions might a person who identifies as bisexual have that are unique in the LGBTQ+ umbrella? (Answer: Discuss double discrimination.)

   i. Why can it be more challenging to find support and community as a bisexual person?

   ii. How might this woman's life experiences change depending on the gender identity of who she is partnered with: a cisgendered man, a woman, a transgender man, and so on?

2. As a music therapist, how might you explore the identity of bisexuality?

3. What musical artists and songs might you include who also identify as bisexual and persons of color, and address the topic of bisexuality?

4. How is this client's intersectional identity of being bisexual and black significant?

CASE SCENARIO 7

You are a music therapist working in a middle school setting. A student you are working with one on one through an individual education plan identifies as queer. She discloses to you that she recently came out to her family. Her father is no longer talking to her. Her mother told her they will not accept her sexual orientation and will kick her out of the house if she "starts dressing like a man." They refuse to accept her identity. They have also told her that she is too young to understand, and that other lesbians at school are influencing her. She states she is afraid they will kick her out and is heartbroken with their response.

Study questions

1. What unique stresses do LGBTQ+ youth face?

2. What does it mean to "come out?"

3. What are some of the concerns and stressors that may be involved in coming out of the closet with:

    i. family

    ii. friends

    iii. work/school

    iv. religious organizations

    v. other community members.

4. What can you do as a music therapist to affirm and validate her identity?

5. What could you do to address her fear and sadness about her family's response?

6. What resources should you have available for her?

Conclusion

It is our hope that the information in this chapter is helpful in expanding the readers' knowledge of LGBTQ+ culture, history, music, and potential music therapy approaches. The unique, and often separate, identities within the LGBTQ+ umbrella, which are a mixture of different sexualities, genders, and intersectional identities, all help create a queer and colorful kaleidoscope lens through which each LGBTQ+ person experiences life. Understanding that LGBTQ+ culture is different from heterosexual cisgender culture, and awareness of the impact of heteronormativity, will deepen one's understanding of LGBTQ+ clients and families.

Recognizing and critically examining our own privilege, power, and value systems on a personal and professional level can enable us to adjust our music therapy practices accordingly (Oswanski & Donnenwerth, 2017). Witnessing, appreciating, and celebrating our LGBTQ+ clients is essential in creating and keeping an open and affirming music therapy practice for all clients, and allows the space for LGBTQ+ clients to feel safe, seen, and accepted.

LGBTQ+ clients will come in and out of your practices, whether you are working with babies, children, teens, adults, or seniors; whether at the beginning of life or the end; whether you are working in schools, hospitals, or private practice; whether they are out and open to you or remain closeted. How you educate yourself, present yourself, and prepare your practice to create a safe, affirming space will have a large impact on your effectiveness as a music therapist.

References

Adler, R., Hirsch, S., & Pickering, J. (eds). (2019). *Voice and Communication Therapy for the Transgender/Gender Diverse Client: A Comprehensive Clinical Guide* (third edition). San Diego, CA: Plural.

Ahessy, B. T. (2011). "Lesbian, gay and bisexual issues in music therapy training and education: The love that dares not sing its name." *Canadian Journal of Music Therapy,* 17(1), 11–33.

American Music Therapy Association (AMTA). (2019). *Code of Ethics.* Retrieved from: www.musictherapy.org/about/ethics.

American Speech-Language-Hearing Association (ASHA) (2019). Retrieved from: www.asha.org/public/speech/disorders/voice-and-communication-change-for-transgender-people.

Andersson, B., Ulvaeus, B., Anderson, S. (1976). "Dancing Queen" [ABBA]. On *Dancing Queen* [vinyl single record]. New York, NY: Atlantic.

Ansdell, G. (2002). "Community music therapy and the winds of change." *Voices: A World Forum for Music Therapy,* 2(2). https://doi.org/10.15845/voices.v2i2.83.

Bain, C., Grzanka, P. R., & Crowe, B.J. (2016). "Toward a queer music therapy: The implications of queer theory for radically inclusive music therapy." *The Arts in Psychotherapy,* 50, 22–33.

Baines, S. (2013). "Music therapy as an anti-oppressive practice." *The Arts in Psychotherapy,* 40(1), 1–5.

Balkin, R. S., Schlosser, L. Z., & Levi, D. H. (2009). "Religious identity and cultural diversity: Exploring the relationships between religious identity, sexism, homophobia, and multicultural competence." *Journal of Counseling & Development,* 87(4), 420–427.

Bidell, M. P. (2005). "The sexual orientation counselor competency scale: Assessing attitudes, skills, and knowledge of counselors working with lesbian, gay, and bisexual clients." *Counselor Education and Supervision,* 44, 267–279. doi:10.1002/j.1556-6978.2005.tb01755.

Bidell, M. P. (2014). "Personal and professional discord: Examining religious conservatism and lesbian-, gay-, and bisexual-affirmative counselor competence." *Journal of Counseling & Development,* 92(2), 170–179. doi:10.1002/j.1556-6676.2014.00145.

Bogan, L. (1935). "BD Women's Blues" [Vinyl record]. Chicago, IL: RST Records.

Boggan, C., Grzanka, P. R., & Bain, C. (2017). "Perspectives on queer music therapy: A qualitative analysis of music therapists' reactions to radically inclusive practice." *Journal of Music Therapy*, 54(4), 375–404.

Bonde, L. O. (2011). "Health musicing—music therapy or music and health? A model, empirical examples and personal reflections." *Music and Arts in Action*, 3(2): 120–138.

Brill, D., Dong-Hwa, C., Kirby, K., Hancock, H., & Davis, J. (1990). "Groove Is in the Heart" [Deee-Lite]. On *World Clique* [CD]. New York, NY: Elektra.

Clarke, V., Bell, A. (1988). "A Little Respect" [Erasure]. On *The Innocents* [CD]. Birmingham, UK: Sire.

Clarke, V., Ellis, S. J., Peel, E., & Riggs, D. W. (2010). *Lesbian Gay Bisexual Trans & Queer Psychology: An Introduction*. New York, NY: Cambridge University Press.

Curtis, S. L. (2012). "Music therapy and social justice: A personal journey." *The Arts in Psychotherapy*, 39(3), 209–213. doi:10.1016/j.aip.2011.12.004.

Curtis, S. L. (2013). "Women Survivors of Abuse and Developmental Trauma." In L. Eyre (ed.), *Guidelines for Music Therapy Practice: Mental Health* (pp.263–268). Philadelphia, PA: Barcelona Publishers.

Curtis, S. L. (2015). "Feminist music therapists in North America: Their lives and their practices." *Voices*, 15(2). https://doi.org/10.15845/voices. v15i2.812.

Curtis, S. L. (2017). "The Intersections of Gender and Culture." In A. Whitehead-Pleaux & X. Tan (ed.), *Cultural Intersections: Music Therapy, Health and the Person* (pp.207–222). Gilsum, NH: Barcelona Publishers.

Deacon, J. (1984). "I Want to Break Free" [Queen]. On *The Works* [Vinyl record]. Los Angeles, CA.: EMI, Capitol.

Diamond, S. (2018). I Am Her [Shea Diamond]. On *Seen It All* [Digital]. Asylum Worldwide LLC.

DiFranco, A. (1995). "32 Flavors" [Ani DiFranco]. On *Not a Pretty Girl* [CD]. Buffalo, NY: Righteous Babe.

Ditto, B., Paine, B., Billie, H. (2009). "Heavy Cross" [Gossip]. On *Music For Men* [CD]. New York, NY: Columbia.

Drescher J. (2015). "Out of DSM: Depathologizing homosexuality." *Behavioral Sciences,* 5(4), 565–575. doi:10.3390/bs5040565.

Edwards, B. & Rodgers, N. (1979). "We Are Family" [Sister Sledge]. On *We Are Family* [Vinyl record]. New York, NY: Cotillion (1978).

Edwards, B. & Rodgers, N. (1980). "I'm Coming Out" [Diana Ross]. On *I'm Coming Out* [Vinyl single record]. New York, NY: Motown. (1979).

Elledge, J. (2010). *Queers in American Popular Culture (2)*. Santa Barbara, CA: Praeger.

Eno, B. & Bowie, D. (1979). "Boys Keep Swinging" [David Bowie]. On *Lodger* [Vinyl record]. New York, NY: RCA.

Etheridge, M. (1993). "Come To My Window" [Melissa Etheridge]. On *Yes I Am* [CD]. Los Angeles, CA: Island.

Farber, J. (2019, Feb 25). *Jackie Shane: Remembering the Groundbreaking Trans Soul Singer*. Retrieved from www.theguardian.com/music/2019/feb/25/jackie-shane-groundbreaking-trans-soul-singer.

Farmer, L. B. (2017). "An examination of counselors' religiosity, spirituality, and lesbian-, gay-, and bisexual- affirmative counselor competence." *Professional Counselor*, 7(2), 114–128. doi:10.15241/lbf.7.2.114.

Fitzsimons, T. (2018, Nov. 14) *Anti-LGBTQ Hate Crimes Rose 3 Percent in '17, FBI Finds*. NBC News. Retrieved from www.nbcnews.com/feature/nbc-out/anti-lgbtq-hate-crimes-rose-3-percent-17-fbi-finds-n936166.

Gallo, M. (2006). *Different Daughters: A History of the Daughters of Bilitis and the Rise of the Lesbian Rights Movement*. New York, NY: Carrol & Graf Publishers.

Gay, Lesbian & Straight Education Network (2016). *Safe Space Kit: Guide to Being an Ally to LGBT Students*. Retrieved from www.glsen.org/sites/default/files/GLSEN Safe Space Kit.pdf.

Germanotta, S. & Laursen, J. (2010). "Born This Way" [Lady Gaga]. On *Born This Way* [CD]. London, UK: Streamline (2011).

Grace, L. J. (2013). "True Trans Soul Rebel" [Against Me!]. On *Transgender Dysphoria Blues* [Digital]. Elkton, FL: Total Treble.

Gumble, M. (2019). Embodied Speech Through Song: A Queer Autoethnographic Exploration of Gender Affirming Voicework in Music Therapy. (Unpublished master's thesis) Slippery Rock University, Slippery Rock, PA. Retrieved from http://uploads.documents.cimpress.io/v1/uploads/411d43a2-b0d5-4e73-9b36-6a8b5af3a3a4~110/original?tenant=vbu-digital.

Hadley, S. (ed.). (2006). *Feminist Perspectives in Music Therapy*. Gilsum, NH: Barcelona Publishers.

Hahna, N. D., & Schwantes, M. (2011). "Feminist music therapy pedagogy: A survey of music therapy educators." *Journal of Music Therapy*, 48(3), 289–316. doi: 10.1093/jmt/48.3.289.

Hanna, K., Karren, B., Vail, T., & Wilcox, K. (1993). "Rebel Girl" [Bikini Kill]. On *Pussy Whipped* [CD]. Seattle WA: Kill Rock Stars.

Hardy, S. (2018). Music therapy and transgender adolescents: A community based workshop to promote wellness. (Unpublished master's thesis) Berklee College of Music, Boston, MA.

Hardy, S. & Whitehead-Pleaux, A. (2017). "The Cultures of the Lesbian, Gay, Bisexual, Transgender, Intersex, and Questioning Communities." In A. Whitehead-Pleaux & X. Tan (eds), *Cultural Intersections in Music Therapy: Music, Health, and the Person*. Gilsum, NH: Barcelona Publishers.

History.com (2017). *The History of AIDS*. Retrieved from www.history.com/topics/1980s/history-of-aids.

Human Rights Campaign (HRC). (2018). *LGBTQ Youth Report*. Washington, DC: Human Rights Campaign. Retrieved from www.hrc.org/resources/2018-lgbtq-youth-report.

Human Rights Campaign (HRC). (2019). *State Laws*. Washington, DC: Human Rights Campaign. Retrieved from www.hrc.org/state-maps/pdf-all.

Human Rights Campaign Foundation (2018). *Dismantling a Culture of Violence: Understanding Anti-Transgender Violence and Ending the Crisis*. Washington, DC: Human Rights Campaign Foundation. Retrieved from https://assets2.hrc.org/files/assets/resources/2018AntiTransViolenceReportSHORTENED.pdf.

Jackson, H. L. & Kremer, B. (2018). *The Singing Teacher's Guide to Transgender Voices*. San Diego, CA: Plural Publishing.

Jagose, A. R. (1996). *Queer Theory: An Introduction*. New York, NY: New York University Press.

Kelly, T. & Steinberg, B. (1986). "True Colors" [Cyndi Lauper]. On *True Colors* [CD]. New York, NY: Portrait.

Kenny, C. B. (2006). *Music & Life in the Field of Play: An Anthology*. Gilsum, NH: Barcelona.

Lambert, M. (2013). "She Keeps Me Warm" [Mary Lambert]. On *Welcome to the Age of My Body* [CD]. Los Angeles, CA: Capitol.

Lang, K. D. & Mink, B. (1991). "Constant Craving" [K.D. Lang]. On *Ingénue* [CD]. Vancouver, British Columbia, Canada: Sire (1992).

Lauper, C., (2013). "Raise You Up" On *Kinky Boots, Original Broadway Cat Recording* [Digital]. New York, NY: Masterworks Broadway.

Lorde, A. (1984). *Sister Outsider: Essays and Speeches*. Trumansburg, NY: Crossing Press.

Lynn, C., Paich, D., & Foster, D. (1978). "Got to Be Real" [Cheryl Lynn] On *Got to Be Real* [Vinyl single record]. Hollywood, CA: Columbia.

Madonna & Pettibone, S. (1989). "Vogue" [Madonna] On *I'm Breathless* [CD]. Los Angeles, CA: Sire (1990).

Marx, R. A. & Kettrey, H. H. (2016). "Gay–Straight alliances are associated with lower levels of school-based victimization of LGBTQ youth: A systematic review and meta-analysis." *Journal of Youth and Adolescence*, 45(7), 1269–1282. doi:10.1007/s10964-016-0501-7.

Michael, G. (1989). "Freedom!'90". On *Listen Without Prejudice Vol. 1*. [CD]. New York, NY: Columbia. (1990).

Mills, M. & Stoneham, G. (2017). *The Voice Book for Trans and Non-Binary People: A Practical Guide to Creating and Sustaining Authentic Voice and Communication*. London: Jessica Kingsley Publishers.

Morali, J. & Willis, V. (1978). "YMCA" [The Village People] On *YMCA* [Vinyl single record]. New York, NY: Casablanca.

Morris, B. J. (n.d.) History of lesbian, gay, bisexual and transgender social movements. *American Psychological Association*. Retrieved from www.apa.org/pi/lgbt/resources/history.

Movement Advancement Project (MAP), Center for American Progress, Human Rights Campaign, Freedom to Work, and National Black Justice Coalition (2013). *A Broken Bargain for LGBT Workers of Color.* Retrieved from www.lgbtmap.org/workers-of-color.

Oswanski, L. & Donnenwerth, A. (2017). "Allies for Social Justice." In A. Whitehead-Pleaux & X. Tan (ed.), *Cultural Intersections: Music Therapy, Health and the Person* (pp.257–270). Gilsum, NH: Barcelona Publishers.

Oswanski, L., Robinson, B., Donnenwerth, A. & Hearns, M. (2019). "Equality for All: The Intersection of Supervision and LGBTQ+ Topics." In M. Forinash (ed.), *Music Therapy Supervision* (second edition). Philadelphia, PA: Barcelona.

Oswanski, L, Whitehead-Pleaux, A., Kynvi, L., Robinson, B., Hardy, S., & Donnenwerth, A. (2018). LGBTQ+ topics explored. AMTA E-Course. Silver Spring, MD: American Music Therapy Association.

Perren, F. & Fekaris, D. (1978). "I Will Survive" [Gloria Gaynor] On *I Will Survive* [Vinyl single record]. Los Angeles, CA: Polydor.

Pezzella, F. S., Fetzer, M. D., & Keller, T. (2019). "The dark figure of hate crime underreporting." *American Behavioral Scientist.* https://doi.org/10.1177/0002764218823844.

Quin, T., Quin, S., & Kurstin, G. (2012). "Closer" [Tegan and Sara]. On *Heartbomb* [Digital]. Vapor: Warner Bros.

Rainey, J. S. & Trusty, J. (2007). "Attitudes of master's-level counseling students toward gay men and lesbians." *Counseling and Values*, 52(1), 12–24. doi:10.1002/j.2161-007X.2007.tb00084.

Rainey, M. (1928). "Prove it On Me Blues" [Vinyl record] Chicago, IL: Paramount.

Robinson, J. M., Michaels, J., Larsson, M., Fredriksson, R., & Tranter, J. (2015-2018) "Make Me Feel" [Janelle Monáe]. On *Dirty Computer* [Digital]. Atlanta, GA: Wondaland, Bad Boy, Atlantic (2018).

RuPaul, Harry, J., & Tee, L. (1992). "Supermodel" (You Better Work [RuPaul]. On *Supermodel of the World* [CD]. New York, NY: Tommy Boy.

Ruud, E. (n.d.). *Community Music Therapy.* Retrieved from www.hf.uio.no/imv/personer/vit/emeriti/evenru/even.artikler/CMTherapy.pdf.

Saliers, E. (1988). Closer to Fine [Indigo Girls]. On *Indigo Girls* [CD]. Los Angeles, CA: Epic (1989).

Sanabria, S. (2012). "Religious orientation and prejudice: Predictors of homoprejudice." *Journal of LGBT Issues in Counseling*, 6(3), 183–201. doi:10.1080/15538605.

Satcher, J. & Schumacker, R. (2009). "Predictors of modern homonegativity among professional school counselors." *Journal of LGBT Issues in Counseling*, 3, 21–36. doi:10.1080/15538600902754452

Seabrook, D. (2019). "Toward a radical practice: A recuperative critique of improvisation in music therapy using intersectional feminist theory." *The Arts in Psychotherapy*, 63, 1–8. doi: 10.1016/j.aip.2019.04.002.

Small, C. (1998). *Musicking: The Meanings of Performing and Listening.* Middletown, CT: Wesleyan University Press.

Social justice. (2019). In *Oxford Online Dictionary*. Retrieved from www.lexico. com/en/definition/social_justice.Stige, B. (2002). *Culture-Centered Music Therapy*. Gilsum, NH, Barcelona.

Stige, B. (2002). *Culture-centered Music Therapy*. Gilsum, NH: Barcelona Publishers.

Sullivan, N. (2003). *A Critical Introduction to Queer Theory*. New York, NY: New York University Press.

The Trevor Project. (2019a). *National Survey on LGBTQ Mental Health*. New York, NY: The Trevor Project.

The Trevor Project. (2019b). *Research Brief: Accepting Adults Reduce Suicide Attempts among LGBTQ Youth*. New York, NY: The Trevor Project.

Trask. S. & Mitchell, J. C., (1999). "The Origin of Love." On *Hedwig and the Angry Inch: Original Cast Recording* [CD]. Atlantic/WEA.

Vaillancourt, G. (2012). "Music therapy: A community approach to social justice." *The Arts in Psychotherapy*, 39(1), 173–178.

Vaughn, S. (1990). "Morality and entertainment: The origins of the motion picture production code." *The Journal of American History*, 77(1), 39–65. doi:10.2307/2078638.

Warren, D. (1989). "If I Could Turn Back Time" [Cher]. On *Heart of Stone* [CD]. Santa Monica, CA: Geffen.

Whitehead-Pleaux, A., Donnenwerth, A., Robinson, B., Hardy, S., *et al.* (2012). "Lesbian, gay, bisexual, transgender, and questioning: Best practices in music therapy." *Music Therapy Perspectives*, 30(2), 158–166.

Whitehead-Pleaux, A., Donnenwerth, A. M., Robinson, B., Hardy, S., *et al.* (2013). "Music therapists' attitudes and actions regarding the LGBTQ+ community: A preliminary report." *Arts in Psychotherapy*, 40(4), 404–414. https://doi.org/10.1016/j.aip.2013.05.006.

Wirrick, J., Sylvester. (1978). "You Make Me Feel (Mighty Real)" [Sylvester]. On *You Make Me Feel (Mighty Real)* [Vinyl single record]. Los Angeles CA: Fantasy Records (1977).

Yardley, W. (2014, May 29). *Storme DeLarverie, Early leader in the gay rights movement, dies at 93*. Retrieved from www.nytimes.com/2014/05/30/ nyregion/storme-delarverie-early-leader-in-the-gay-rights-movement-dies-at-93.html.

York, E. (2015). "Inclusion of Lesbian, Gay, Bisexual, Transgender, Questioning Content into the Music Therapy Curriculum: Resources for the Educator." In K. D. Goodman (ed.), *International Perspectives in Music Therapy Education and Training* (pp.241–266). Springfield, IL: Thomas.

CHAPTER 4

Exploring Aging Through a Multicultural Lens

Melita Belgrave, PhD, MT-BC

On first glance, you might assume that I identify as an African American woman who was born in the United States. However, after getting to know me you would know that I was born in the United States after both my mother and father migrated from Belize, located in Central America, and that I identify as being a Belizean woman who was born in the United States. Although I grew up state-side, I definitely lived in a traditional Belizean multigenerational home. My maternal grandmother lived with us and was my earliest friend. She cooked for me, watched TV with me, and played with me while my parents were at work during the day. We listened to Belizean music in our home and ate traditional Belizean meals. There was a strong Belizean community in Chicago, so I grew up around other Belizean friends who lived the same culture and traditions that I did. Many of the homes I spent time in as a kid and teen were multigenerational. Looking back, it makes sense that I would be drawn to working with older adults and creating intergenerational programs, since that is how I grew up. Many of my memories with my immediate and extended family include music-making experiences (my paternal grandmother insisted that the grandchildren learn to play the piano), with either cousins or uncles playing the piano and everyone singing. Additionally, all events and gatherings included recorded music and at some point in time there was multigenerational dancing, including the youngest and oldest family members.

I remember the first time that I thought about culture and aging while I was observing a music session in graduate school. The room was made up of mostly white older adults, with a few black older adults. Yet the music was the same as if there was a room of only white older adults. In that moment, I thought to myself what would it look like if my parents were present for the session. What assumptions would a music therapist or entertainer make about them? Would the therapist assume that they were black older adults who grew up in the south and liked Baptist music? If so, the initial assumption would be wrong because my parents are Belizean immigrants who migrated in their early 20s. They grew up Protestant and they enjoy all types of music, including classical, ragtime, jazz, soca, calypso, and more. This observation experience made me really think about the assumptions we make when scanning a room of older adults, and that we tend to categorize older adults by their illness or their preferred music genre but that is it. Yet is this really reflective of the whole person? What more do I need to consider as a therapist?

Background

Today there are over 44 million people living in the United States who are labeled as foreign born, meaning they were born outside the United States. The individuals categorized as foreign born comprise 12.9 percent of the population. This is an increase from the 1970s where 9.6 million people (4.7 percent) were labeled as foreign born. Currently, the largest population of foreign-born individuals migrate from Mexico (25 percent) followed by India and China (6 percent), Philippines, (5 percent), El Salvador, Vietnam, Cuba, and Dominican Republic (3 percent), South Korea and Guatemala (2 percent) (Zong, Batalova, & Burrows, 2019).

In a recent migration policy report (Zong *et al.*, 2019), it was found that "over 66 million people in the United States speak a language other than English in their home" (p.7). The most common language spoken in homes is Spanish (62 percent). Other languages include Chinese, Tagalog, Vietnamese, Arabic, French, Korean, Russian, German, Haitian Creole, Hindi, Portuguese, Italian, Polish, and Urdu. Sixteen percent of the immigrant population are aged 65 and older (Zong *et al.*, 2019).

With the growing number of immigrants and diversity within the immigrant population across languages spoken and countries where persons migrate from, there is a good chance that music therapists will work with clients who are different from them. It is important for music therapists to apply a multicultural lens when working with older adult populations. This chapter will explore the literature related to multiculturalism, music therapy, and aging. Additionally, this chapter contains learning activities related to the literature on music therapy experiences with older adults utilizing a multicultural lens.

Multiculturalism in music therapy

Multicultural aspects in music therapy have been explored since the 1990s with early writings by Bradt (1997) as well as Darrow and Molloy (1998). These early writings focused on developing a lens and framework for multicultural music therapy practice. Bradt (1997) introduced music therapists to multicultural counseling theories and how those theories could be used as a framework for music therapy. Darrow and Molloy (1998) explored how educational training occurred for music therapy students and clinicians. Findings revealed that students received training in elective and general education courses. The majority of clinicians shared that they received training through experience as a music therapist, and that they did not receive enough training in school on multicultural music or working with clients from other cultures.

More music therapists continued to contribute to the literature by expanding on earlier frameworks from models utilized in other professions like multicultural counseling (Brown, 2001). Whereas other music therapists began to explore the use of multicultural music therapy in the United States and other countries (Chase, 2003; Valentino, 2006), Brown (2001) expanded on earlier writings by defining terms related to multiculturalism. Brown (2001) also shared the importance of being a culturally centered therapist and having cultural empathy in music therapy practice. Additionally, Brown introduced a new model that could be used in music therapy: the ADDRESSING model developed by Hays (1996). Each letter of the word ADDRESSING represents a cultural category: "A—Age and generational influences, D—Developmental disability, D—Disability acquired later in life, R—Religion and spiritual orientation, E—Ethnicity/race identity, S—Socio-economic status, S—Sexual orientation, I—Indigenous heritage, N—National origin, and G—Gender" (Hays, 2013, pp.15–16).

In 2003, Chase continued to contribute to the literature by reviewing the multicultural music therapy literature in the United States and Canada. In addition to providing the review, Chase provided steps for clinicians to explore inside and outside music therapy sessions to improve their multicultural lens and flexibility when working with diverse clients. Valentino (2006) conducted a descriptive study to explore cross-cultural empathy for music therapists in Australia and America. Results revealed that music therapists who received cross-cultural training in their academic programs were rated with a higher level of cross-cultural empathy compared to music therapists who did not receive cross-cultural training in school.

As the area of multicultural music therapy continues to grow, more clinicians are developing research articles, book chapters, and textbooks which share steps that clinicians can take to strengthen their multicultural journey and lens. The steps include:

> moving beyond a one-dimensional lens of culture, such as repertoire or language, into a multidimensional lens which includes a variety of aspects within an individual's culture such as the meaning of medicine and wellbeing, the meaning and function of music, worldviews and historical realities, and diversity within the culture. (Belgrave, 2017, p.473)

Additionally, authors encourage music therapists to be aware of their own biases and assumptions regarding their culture and other cultures. Other steps also include being aware of the various categories of culture, including culture of heritage, culture of religion, culture of generation, culture of location, and culture of identity, and how these categories affect the therapeutic relationship for the client and the therapist (Goelst, 2016; Hadley & Norris, 2015; Kim & Whitehead-Pleaux, 2015; Olsen, 2017; Stige, 2015; Whitehead-Pleaux & Tan, 2017).

Multiculturalism in music therapy with older adults

Music therapy for older adults is a topic that has been well researched and documented in research articles and textbooks (Belgrave *et al.*, 2011; Clair & Memmott, 2008; Clair & Davis, 2008; Ridder & Wheeler, 2015; Wilhelm & Cevasco-Trotter, 2018). This literature focuses on the benefits to older adults in wellness settings, older adults diagnosed with dementia and Alzheimer's disease, older adults in intergenerational settings, and older adults in palliative care and hospice settings. A review of the literature related to aging and music therapy is beyond the scope of this chapter, due to the lack of multicultural topics within the literature. I chose to review articles related to multicultural music therapy and aging.

One of the topics related to multicultural music therapy and aging is the application of various theories of aging in the music therapy setting (Cohen, 2014; Wheeler, 2015). Aging is often associated with declines and losses, and there is an early theory of aging related to the concept of loss. It was believed that aging could be described with the disengagement theory, where older adults become withdrawn as they age. Another early theory combatted the idea of disengagement with activity theory, where healthy aging was measured by how active an older adult was. Cohen (2014) explored both of these theories as well as additional sociological aging theories and then created strategies for the music therapist to use while employing each of the aging theories. One of the tenets of using a multicultural lens in music therapy is seeing the client as a whole person and recognizing the influence of a person's culture on how they engage in the therapeutic process. There are two sociological theories of aging that relate to this tenet: the continuity theory and age-stratification theory.

Practitioners who utilize the continuity theory view the role of older adults' social lives as an important factor. This theory supports the idea that older adults cope with aging by maintaining the social roles and experiences that they held during the age range of 45–65. Cohen (2014) shares several strategies that music therapists might adapt if they are working with older adult clients and utilizing the continuity theory. Practitioners who utilize the age-stratification theory view the role of older adults' lived experiences in a historical context and the effect that those lived experiences have on the therapeutic process and relationship. This theory supports the idea that older adults experience aging with the lens of their past historical experiences. Therefore, every generation of older adults would be different in how they approach aging because their lived experiences at any point in their life would be different and would have affected them in the past differently, based on their age. Cohen (2014) shared several strategies that music therapists might employ if they are working with older adults in a setting that utilizes the age-stratification theory. For more information on applying the strategies located in the article please see Learning Activity 9 later in the chapter (Cohen, 2014).

There is a small literature base pertaining to multiculturalism, music therapy, and aging. A further exploration of this literature reveals that the majority of research articles have been conducted in Australia with older adults who are categorized as culturally and linguistically diverse. Music therapy sessions have happened in group settings and individual sessions (Baker & Grocke, 2009; Chan, 2014; Forrest, 2000; Ip-Winfield & Grocke, 2011; Ip-Winfield, Wen, & Queena, 2014; Lauw, 2016; Mondanaro, 2016; Shapiro, 2005). Forrest (2000) conducted a case study on an older adult woman receiving music therapy while in hospice care. The patient resided in Australia as an adult, but she was from Russia and also spent time in England. As part of the music therapy sessions, the patient identified that she enjoyed a variety of musical styles including Western classical, popular, and film music. During the early music therapy sessions, the music therapist played music from the genres requested by the client. The client actively engaged in the sessions and shared verbal responses of what she liked about the music. However, once the patient's health declined she exhibited physical signs of distress such as difficulty breathing, verbal expressions of not having enough time, and decreased orientation to time, place, and person. The music therapist interviewed the patient's sister about their past and discovered that the patient and her sister were forced to leave Russia during World War II as young women. They moved to England while waiting for the rest of their family to join them. Unfortunately, their family members did not survive and the patient and her sister migrated to Australia. The patient's sister shared that they never spoke about their migration story. They talked about their childhood but never discussed or shared the music of their childhood, although music was a large part of their growing-up experience and included Russian folk and classical music. The music therapist suggested bringing in music from the patient's childhood to assist with processing memories and feelings associated with childhood and her migration story.

When cultural music from the patient's past was brought into the session the patient actively engaged in the session through singing and verbally processing her migration story. She expressed her feelings and memories surrounding that time in her life. This included feelings of loss associated with family members and difficulty adjusting to a new life in Australia. The music therapy session included the patient's sister, as well as the daughter and granddaughter of the patient. This case study demonstrates the benefit of viewing an older adult client through a multicultural lens. There were memories and feelings that the patient needed to process for herself as well as with family members. Finding a safe space to unlock those memories and feelings occurred because of the music therapist's journey and willingness to explore the patient's culture (Forrest 2000).

Other researchers (Baker & Grocke, 2009; Ip-Winfield & Grocke, 2011) explored the experiences of music therapists working in Australia with older adults who were categorized as culturally and linguistically diverse through descriptive studies. The authors of both studies examined the music repertoire and music therapy interventions used by music therapists when working with clients who are of different cultures and speak different primary languages from the therapist. The researchers found that clients who were categorized as culturally and linguistically diverse had different levels of engagement in a music therapy session depending on their cultural background. Some older adults from certain backgrounds were more observably engaged, whereas others were more reserved in their engagement. Engagement included active singing, culturally specific greetings, and various forms of non-verbal communication. Music therapy methods and interventions that were easy to implement were receptive, improvisation, reminiscence, music listening (recorded and live), instrument playing, and movement-based interventions. This could be possibly due to the limited use of language needed to participate in many of those interventions. Similarly, songwriting was shown to be difficult for clients with limited English proficiency. Additional lessons learned when providing music therapy sessions for older adults utilizing a multicultural lens included:

- Building rapport takes time, which makes sense if a therapist is taking an approach of understanding someone's culture and the role it plays in their life.

- The use of non-verbal communication is important, and music therapists suggested learning a few greetings, words and/or phrases in the language of the older adult clients to ease communication.

- It's important to research the use of music in the clients' culture.

- Music therapists need to understand the use of personal space and boundaries as they relate to the client's culture.

The remaining research articles describe music therapy programs delivered in individual settings that utilize a multicultural lens. Music therapists demonstrated cultural empathy and openness to other cultures by gathering information from their clients pertaining to culture, values, beliefs, and languages. In a sense, this went beyond what type of music the client liked to who the client was as a result of the culture they grew up in. Music therapists found that client benefits included an increased sense of self and identity, and improved cognitive, physical, psychosocial, and communication skills (Chan, 2014; Ip-Winfield, Wen, & Queena, 2014; Lauw, 2016; Mondanaro, 2016; Shapiro, 2005).

In one study (Chan, 2014), the therapist learned the role of music in the client's culture (German). Although the music therapist did not typically sing in German, she learned the German folk songs that were important to the client. They also co-wrote hello and goodbye songs in German. The therapist shared that using music that was culturally important to the client provided an opportunity for self-identity and connection to her culture and home country. The therapist also shared the importance of learning the influence of the client's culture on help-seeking and coping behaviors for the client, as these vary across different cultures. In one instance, asking for help was seen as a loss and decline, and therefore the client was only able to ask for help when she was in severe pain.

Additionally, researchers have encouraged music therapists to identify other hidden rules or norms for cultures that affect *how* an older adult shows up to a music therapy session or even *if* the older client shows up for a therapy session. One researcher found that the way an older adult was invited to the session and who initiated the invitation contributed to whether or not the older adult would participate in and attend the music therapy session. Also, how the older adult was addressed in the sessions mattered; some older adults preferred a formal greeting, i.e. Mr. or Mrs., or something else that showed respect (Lauw, 2016).

Learning activities

This section contains a series of learning activities that can be completed as stand-alone assignments or in-class modules related to multicultural music therapy and aging.

Learning activity 1: Who am I musically?

Background: This learning activity is based on the reading "Music Therapy and Cultural Diversity" by Seung-A Kim and Annette Whitehead-Pleaux (2015). First, read the chapter, and then begin the learning activity. This activity will assist you in exploring the relationship between your music preference and your culture of location, culture of heritage, culture of generation, culture of religion, and culture of identity. Answer the questions below.

Step 1

- Where are all the places you have lived? (Location)

- Where were your parents born and where did they grow up? (Heritage)

- Where were your grandparents born and where did they grow up? (Heritage)

- Is there a history of immigration in your family? If so, please describe. (Generation)

- What decade where you born in? What decade/years were you as a teenager? What decade/years were you in your 20s? (Generation)

- Has religion, faith, or spirituality played a role in your life? If so, please describe. (Religion)

- What songs, styles/genres, artists, instruments, musical experiences are associated with your culture of heritage, location, generation, and religion?

- Are there any other musical traditions or experiences that your family did/does together? (Heritage, generation, location, religion)

- What music do you listen to now and why? (Identity)

Step 2

Create a visual representation that describes the effect of your culture on your musical preferences. Remember to be creative. You must include at least three of the five categories of culture:

- culture of heritage

- culture of location

- culture of generation

- culture of religion

- culture of identity.

Step 3

If using as a class assignment, have students bring a hard copy or digital copy of their visual representation to share with their classmates. Use the following questions for group discussion.

- What did you learn about yourself?

- What was easy, and what was difficult to complete for the project?

- How can you use this activity as an assessment intervention?

- How else could you use this activity in a music therapy setting?

Learning activity 2: My view on aging

Background: This activity is based on the reading the article "Music therapy and sociological theories of aging" by Nicki S. Cohen (2014). This activity will assist you in identifying your personal experience with aging and how that influences your views on aging theories and perception of aging. Read the article and then complete the steps below.

Step 1

- Think about the relationship and experiences you had with your grandparents and any other older adults in your life.

- List any experiences that you had with both your maternal and paternal grandparents. Also, be sure to include if you did not have a relationship with your maternal or paternal grandparents.

- Do the same thing for any other older adults in your life.

- What are the lessons that you learned from your grandparents or other older adults in your life as a child, teen, and young adult?

- Identify which sociological theories of aging from the article relate to the relationship, experiences, and/or life lessons that you had with grandparents or other older adults in your life.

Learning activity 3: Musical expansions

Background: This activity is based on the reading the article "Challenges of working with people aged 60–75 years from culturally and linguistically diverse groups: Repertoire and music therapy approaches employed by Australian music therapists" by Felicity Baker and Denise Grocke (2009). This activity will assist you in expanding your multicultural musical repertoire for older adults. Read the article and then complete the steps below.

Step 1

- Table 6 contains patriotic songs, Table 7 contains folk songs, and Table 9 contains Italian, Greek, Polish, Chinese, German, Dutch, Russian, Spanish, Yugoslavian, and French songs. Choose a total of two songs from Tables 6, 7, or 9 to add to your repertoire list.

- Explore the background of the song utilizing the bullets below.

  - What is the history of the song (culture, time period)?

  - Who wrote the song?

  - Who popularized the song?

  - Have other artists sung or covered the song? If so, who?

- Explore the music of the song using the bullets below.

  - What is the song structure?

  - What is the key of the song?

  - What chords are in the song?

  - What general instruments are in the song?

  - Does a group or an individual perform the song?

  - What parts of the song will be easy to sing?

  - What parts of the song may be difficult to sing?

  - What parts of the song will be easy to replicate?

- What drives the song (the lyrics, chord structure, rhythm, etc.)?

- How can you replicate that in your arrangement of the song (accompaniment pattern, accompaniment instrument, etc.)?

Learning activity 4: Translation and language learning

Background: This learning activity will assist you in developing phrases that are useful in a music therapy session when working with clients who speak another primary language besides English.

Step 1

- Find three free translator apps and/or websites. Choose a language and begin to develop greetings and phrases related to music in different languages.

Step 2

- Compare and contrast your selected resources by creating a pros and cons list with five to ten points for each app and/or website.

Learning activity 5: Technology bridges music around the world

Background: There are several apps that broadcast radio stations from around the world. This learning activity will assist you in developing technology resources that can be used to develop interventions for clients.

Step 1

- Download the *TuneIn* app and use the browse icon to explore radio stations from around the world.

Step 2

- What are two ways that you could use this in a session?

  - What would be the benefit to the client?

- How could you create interventions for the client to complete when you aren't present?

  - What would be the benefit to the client?

Step 3

- Find two more apps and complete Step 1 and Step 2 with each app.

Learning activity 6: Cultural norms

Background: This activity is based on the reading the article "Mianzi and other social influences on music therapy for older Chinese people in Australian aged care" by Eta Lauw (2016) and the chapter "Music Therapy and Cultural Diversity" by Seung-A Kim and Annette Whitehead-Pleaux (2015). Review the readings and answer the questions below.

Step 1

- Select one of the following cultures to explore for yourself: culture of heritage, culture of location, culture of religion, culture of generation, or culture of identity.

- What are cultural norms from your selected culture related to music engagement, inviting people to a group setting, measuring active engagement, leading an intervention, and so on?

- What are cultural norms from your selected culture related to aging?

- How would the cultural norms affect the way you might structure an individual and a group music therapy session with older adults?

Learning activity 7: Case scenarios and strategies for implementing sociological theories of aging

Background: This activity is based on the reading the article "Music therapy and sociological theories of aging" by Nicki S. Cohen (2014). This activity will assist you in developing music therapy programming and strategies for older adults in wellness settings and assisted living or nursing homes, utilizing the continuity theory. Read the article and then complete the steps below.

Step 1

- Read the strategies for music therapists in the continuity theory section.

Step 2

- Case scenario: You are working as a music therapist with older adults in a wellness setting. Determine the setting and type of music therapy experience you will develop. Utilizing ideas from Consideration 1, develop two to four roles and experiences that could be used in the group. (Think about potential musical and non-musical leadership roles.)

- How could you develop assessment materials to gather information needed to define client roles and music therapy experiences?

Step 3

- Case scenario: You are working as a music therapist with older adults in an assisted living or nursing home setting. Determine the setting and type of music therapy experience you will develop. Utilizing ideas from Consideration 1, develop two to four roles and experiences that could be used in the group. (Think about potential musical and non-musical leadership roles.)

- How could you develop assessment materials to gather information needed to define client roles and music therapy experiences?

Step 4

- Case scenario: Refer to the Consideration 2 section from the article and your notes from Step 2 and Step 3. Develop three questions that will assist you in exploring older adult clients' heritage traditions that would affect their willingness to participate in your music experience, and two of the roles you created from Step 2.

- Develop three questions that will assist you in exploring older adult clients' heritage traditions that would affect their willingness to participate in your music experience, and two of the roles you created from Step 3.

References

Baker, F. & Grocke, D. (2009). "Challenges of working with people aged 60–75 years from culturally and linguistically diverse groups: Repertoire and music therapy approaches employed by Australian music therapists." *Australian Journal of Music Therapy*, 20, 30–55.

Belgrave, M. (2017). "Book Review" [Review of the book *Cultural Intersections in Music Therapy: Music, Health, and the Person*, edited by A. Whitehead-Pleaux & X. Tan]. *Nordic Journal of Music Therapy*, 26(5), 473, doi:10.108 0/08098131.2017.1343372.

Belgrave, M., Darrow, A. A., Walworth, D., & Wlodarczyk, N. (2011). *Music Therapy and Geriatric Populations: A Handbook for Practicing Music Therapists and Healthcare Professionals*. Silver Spring, MD: American Music Therapy Association.

Bradt, J. (1997). "Ethical issues in multicultural counseling: Implications for the field of music therapy." *The Arts in Psychotherapy*, 24(2), 137–143.

Brown, J. M. (2001). "Towards a culturally centered music therapy practice." *Canadian Journal of Music Therapy*, 8(1), 11–24.

Chan, G. (2014). "Cross-cultural music therapy in community aged-care: A case vignette of a CALD elderly woman." *Australian Journal of Music Therapy*, 25, 92–102.

Chase, K. M. (2003). "Multicultural music therapy: A review of literature." *Music Therapy Perspectives*, 21, 84–88. Retrieved from https://academic.oup.com/mtp/article-abstract/21/2/84/1004417 by Arizona State University user on 08 July 2019.

Clair, A. A. & Davis, W. B. (2008). "Music Therapy and Elderly Populations." In W. B. Davis, K. E. Gfeller, & M. H. Thaut (eds), *An introduction to Music Therapy Theory and Practice* (third edition) (pp.181–208). Silver Spring, MD: American Music Therapy Association.

Clair, A. A., & Memmott, J. (2008). *Therapeutic Uses of Music with Older Adults* (second edition). Silver Spring, MD: American Music Therapy Association.

Cohen, N. (2014). "Music therapy and sociological theories of aging." *Music Therapy Perspectives*, 32(1), 84–92. doi:10.1093/mtp/miu01.

Darrow, A. A. & Molloy, D. (1998). "Multicultural perspectives in music therapy: An examination of the literature, educational curricula, and clinical practices in culturally diverse cities of the United States." *Music Therapy Perspectives*, 16, 27–32. Retrieved from https://academic.oup.com/mtp/article-abstract/16/1/27/1080144 by Arizona State University user on 08 July 2019.

Forrest, L.C. (2000). "Addressing issues of ethnicity and identity in palliative care through music therapy practice." *The Australian Journal of Music Therapy*, 11, 23–37.

Goelst, I. L. (2016). *Multicultural Music Therapy: A Manual on Cultural Sensitivity in Music Therapy Practice* (master's thesis). Retrieved from ProQuest (10120790).

Hadley, S. & Norris, M. S. (2015). "Musical multicultural competency in music therapy: The first step." *Music Therapy Perspectives*, 34(2), 129–137. doi:10.1093/mtp/miv045.

Hays, P. A. (1996). "Addressing the complexities of a culture and gender in counseling." *Journal of Counseling and Development*, 74(4), 332–337.

Hays, P. A. (2001). *Addressing Cultural Complexities in Practice: A Framework for Clinicians and Counselors*. Washington, DC: American Psychological Association.

Hays, P. A. (2013). *Connecting Across Cultures: The Helper's Toolkit*. Thousand Oaks, CA: Sage Publications.

Ip-Winfield, V. & Grocke, D. (2011). "Group music therapy methods in cross-cultural aged care practice in Australia." *Australian Journal of Music Therapy*, 22, 59–78.

Ip-Winfield, V., Wen, Y., & Queena, Y. C. (2014). "Home-based music therapy for the aged Chinese community in Melbourne: Challenges and outcomes." *Australian Journal of Music Therapy*, 25, 122–134.

Kim, S. A. & Whitehead-Pleaux, A. (2015). "Music Therapy and Cultural Diversity." In B. Wheeler (ed.), *Music Therapy Handbook* (pp.51–63) New York, NY: Guilford Press.

Lauw, E. (2016). "Mianzi and other social influences on music therapy for older Chinese people in Australian aged care." *Australian Journal of Music Therapy*, 27, 57–68.

Mondanaro, J. F. (2016). "Multiculturally focused medical music psychotherapy in affirming identity to facilitate optimal coping during hospitalization." *Music Therapy Perspectives*, 34(2), 154–160.

Olsen, K. (2017). *Multicultural Music Therapy: Developing Cultural Competency for Students and Young Professionals* (master's thesis). Retrieved from ProQuest (10271675).

Ridder, H. M. & Wheeler, B. (2015). "Music Therapy for Older Adults." In B. Wheeler (ed.), *Music Therapy Handbook* (pp.367–378) New York, NY: Guilford Press.

Shapiro, N. (2005). "Sounds in the world: Multicultural influences in music therapy in clinical practice and training." *Music Therapy Perspectives*, 23(1), 29–35.

Stige, B. (2015). "Culture-Centered Music Therapy." In J. Edwards (ed.), *The Oxford Handbook of Music Therapy* (pp.538–556). New York, NY: Oxford University Press.

Valentino, R. E. (2006). "Attitudes towards cross-cultural empathy in music therapy." *Music Therapy Perspectives*, 24, 108–114. Retrieved from https://academic.oup.com/mtp/article-abstract/24/2/108/1125006 by Arizona State University user on 08 July 2019.

Wheeler, B. L. (ed.) (2015). *Music Therapy Handbook*. New York, NY: Guilford Press.

Whitehead-Pleaux, A. & Tan. X. (eds). (2017). *Multicultural Intersections: Music, Health, and the Person*. Gilsum, NH: Barcelona Publishers.

Wilhelm, L. A. & Cevasco-Trotter, A. M. (2018). "Music Therapy with Older Adults." In A. Knight, B. LaGasse, & A. Clair (eds), *Music Therapy an Introduction to the Profession* (pp.373–394) New York, NY: Guilford Press.

Zong, J., Batalova, J., & Burrows, M. (2019). *Frequently Requested Statistics on Immigrants and Immigration in the United States*. Retrieved from www.migrationpolicy.org/article/frequently-requested-statistics-immigrants-and-immigration-united-states.

CHAPTER 5

Dance and Movement Across Cultures

Natasha Thomas, PhD, MT-BC

CASE SCENARIO

There is a phenomenon I frequently experience when co-facilitating with non-Black colleagues in classrooms of predominantly Black/ African American teens, particularly during drum-based experiences that are rooted in playing West African rhythms on African-style drums. A popular goal with this population is to increase "appropriate" social interaction skills, such as collaboration and turn taking, but often I find the definition of "appropriate" is culturally bound. Specifically, I often observe when musicking with Black participants that they seem to fluidly shift between tapping a foot or two along with their instrument playing and rising to their feet to enter the center of the playing space and move to the beat. This never seems to me to disrupt the flow of the group—in fact, fellow participants often seem to encourage it, with clapping and even verbal cheers to urge the moving participant onwards.

Yet, non-Black co-facilitators often seem uncomfortable with these mannerisms, insisting instead that participants remain seated in their chairs throughout the entirety of the experience, sometimes even shouting over the beat of the music for individuals to "stay in your seats please," whenever they get up, or utilizing sweeping gestures for dancers to move away from the center of the space and find their chairs. To these facilitators, such movement is not considered an "appropriate" social interactive skill. But, more often than not, when Black participants are forced to remain seated and more or less "still" during playing experiences, they generally seem frustrated by this. I've observed participants waving dismissingly or glaring at my co-facilitators after being instructed to return to their seats, and/or resuming playing with a flattened affect from what they had displayed before while moving. Some might just return to their seats but not resume playing at all, leading me to wonder: How is this apparently more "appropriate" interaction in any way better than what was happening before? Is the loss of that individual's participation on the whole worth it to have them meet that measure?

Study questions

1. What underlying assumption is being made by non-Black co-facilitators who insist that Black students stay in their seats throughout drumming experiences?

2. What is lost for Black participants by co-facilitators insisting on in-seat engagement? What might be gained if the co-facilitator encourages their unique form of out-of-seat engagement?

3. How might such experiences be conducted differently so that participants could still reach their goals while being more meaningfully engaged? What information might you need to know to do this?

In this chapter, we will explore various traditions across the world relating to the movement of the body in conjunction with the music that we as music therapists might be bringing into our sessions. But first, we'll begin with defining some key terms and investigating those elements of our field that interact with the field of dance and movement therapy, in order to carefully distinguish our scope of practice in the context of movement, and most competently discuss how we might be more sensitive to the traditions and experiences of the individuals we serve.

Music and movement

The act of "musicking," a term that may be familiar to some proponents of community music therapy (Ansdell, 2002), was originally defined by musicologist Christopher Small in 1998 as "to take part, in any capacity, in a musical performance" (p.9). In elaborating on this definition, Small makes a point of including dance and movement as capacities in which one can take part in music, given that movement can, and often does, in fact, contribute to the atmosphere being created. Small further expands on this definition to include listening and even rehearsing or practicing as elements of musicking, essentially asserting it as an active process that is distinct from the product of music itself. This definition may be helpful in this chapter as we further investigate how the *products* that we as music therapists may present in terms of intentionally organized or improvised sound may interact with the *process* of movement of the human body, whether in the most basic forms of posture (how one "holds" oneself) or the more socialized forms of what many call dance (organized or improvised intentional movement).

Movement and music heavily feature as complementary components in several theoretical foundations of music therapy, including improvisational music therapy (Bruscia, 2014), and analytic music therapy (Eschen, 2002). Research in music therapy generally supports the idea that music serves as a motivator for movement and can aid motor functioning (Clark, Baker, & Taylor, 2012; DeBedaut & Wardon, 2006; Kwake, 2007). One of the most overtly connected music therapy interventions related to movement is Rhythmic Auditory Stimulation, or RAS, which is a neurologic music therapy technique where external auditory stimuli are presented as a means of encouraging the body to regulate its movements to an external beat (Kwake, 2007). Outside neurologic music therapy, however, there is limited research relating to any specific kind of movement that is either encouraged or recognized as an influence in music therapy. Similarly, there is research in dance/movement therapy to support the idea that music choices do influence the types of movements that individuals present (open versus closed posturing, etc., Stahl, 2003). Even if an individual has a limited movement capability, there is evidence to support the fact that the observation of movement can improve memory and emotional state (Cross *et al.*, 2012).

Distinctions between music therapy and dance/movement therapy

With breath at the start of life is both movement and sound, which history tells us even the earliest civilizations recognized and sought to understand (Chaiklin & Wengrower, 2009). Gesture and the earliest attempts to produce and amplify sounds were thus utilized not only as ritual to honor life but as practical attempts to influence the living environment. During the early 20th Century, as dancers like Isadora Duncan and Ruth St. Denis were attempting to bring a semblance of this earlier life–body connection to the contemporary dance world, performers like Marian Chace (who studied under Ruth St. Denis) began to notice that an increasing number of students who were not at all interested in performance were taking classes on these re-emerging forms of expression. This paralleled the rise of psychotherapists like Jung and Freud, and before long, Chase was working in a hospital for returning veterans of World War I, where the field of dance therapy's history begins to sound very familiar to that of music therapy. In those early days, the waltz was often used as a means of opening the space for movement, since it seemed heavily connected to the memories of patients Chase was working with at the time (Chaiklin & Wengrower, 2009). Since Chase's era, dance/movement therapists have worked with both structured and unstructured musical pieces, or no music at all, in order to address a variety of clinical domains through movement.

Dance/movement therapy is defined as the "psychotherapeutic use of movement to promote emotional, social, cognitive and physical integration of the individual" (American Dance Therapy Association, 2018). Registered dance/movement therapists (R-DMTs) practice in a variety of clinical settings with a diverse array of populations and needs, and work within a core therapeutic relationship similar to music therapists, but they use movement as the primary means of assessment and intervention. The use of the term "primary" is important to note here, as analytic music therapists may also make *general* assessments of a session participant's posture and movement as they relate to the process of musicking (Eschen, 2002). Similarly, music therapists trained in the Bonny Method of guided imagery with music may also be familiar with some body-based assessment as it relates to the musicking experience (Viega, 2009); however, even in those session structures, as with most music therapy, the body is part of a musical whole, with music as the primary source of assessment information and means of addressing participant needs.

Examples of differing assessment foci

Dance/movement therapist Judith Kestenberg is recognized in the field for her creation of the Kestenberg Movement Profile, or KMP, which is one of several assessment tools widely used by R-DMTs. The profile is based on a rhythmic paradigm that mirrors Freud's psychosexual theory of development, from the oral stages of infancy to the more genital stages of 5- and 6-year-olds (Loman, 2016). Similar to Freud's theories, these stages have been considered by many to be universal, with subconscious pathology being indicated if someone appears "stuck" in a particular stage or pattern. As with most prominent constructs familiar to both music and dance/movement therapists, however, these perspectives are undoubtedly Western in nature, and worthy of questioning (Hadley & Thomas, 2018). It can never be guaranteed that any one theory, perspective, or profile will be universally applicable across all cultures and traditions, thus this particular profile (the KMP) is not presented in any sort of definitive way here, but rather as a framework from which we can further discuss the distinction between how registered dance/movement therapists and music therapists view and integrate movement into the treatment process.

According to the KMP, individual movement vocabulary begins as early as the fetal stages of development, with healthy individuals progressing through a series of "tension flow" rhythms that are either "indulging" or "fighting," across developmental levels. An overview of the KMP, adapted to include developmental ages as parallels from Freud's psychosexual stages of development where those exist, is provided in Table 5.1. Please note that the latter two stages are

unique to the KMP and do not have developmental correlations to
Freud's theory of stages.

Table 5.1: An overview of the Kestenberg Movement Profile

Phase	Indulging rhythms	Fighting rhythms
Oral (birth to 1 year)	Sucking	Snapping/Biting
Anal (1 to 3 years)	Twisting	Strain/Release
Urethral (3 to 6 years)	Running/Drifting	Starting/Stopping
Inner genital	Swaying	Surging/Birthing
Outer genital	Jumping	Spurting/Ramming

In discussing the KMP with some practicing R-DMTs, it would seem
that the rhythmic terms utilized above are universally understood
among them, but many music therapists (myself included!) may
find they need further explanation. Visually notated examples of
the rhythms included in the KMP have been conducted by Longstaff
(2007) and are available online. I've taken the liberty of interpreting
those notations for more auditory mediums in Figure 5.1.

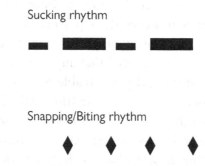

Sucking rhythm

Snapping/Biting rhythm

FIGURE 5.1: MUSICAL INTERPRETATIONS OF THE
KESTENBERG PROFILE RHYTHMS

The above example would suggest that the term "sucking" might
almost be considered to represent a fluid, steady, and regulated
rhythm, similar to a heartbeat (Shree, 2018). By contrast then, the
snapping/biting rhythm would seem perhaps still steady, but more
prone to dysregulation, with sharp, singular beats that may have no
reverberation at all.

In considering the KMP, many certified music therapists (MT-BCs) may find themselves thinking of Bruscia's Improvisation Assessment Profile, or IAP (2001), which is presented in Table 5.2.

Table 5.2: An overview of Brusica's (2001)
Improvisation Assessment Profile

Profile		
Autonomy	Dependent	Independent
Variability	Rigid	Highly variable
Integration	Irregular	Well integrated
Salience	Unstable	Stable
Tension	Strained	Relaxed
Congruence	Disconnected	Connected

Here, we can see some parallels, in that individual profiles in the IAP, similar to Kestenberg's stages, can exist along a spectrum of presentation. One might say, in interpreting an individual utilizing the KMP, that the "sucking" rhythm is operating with what Bruscia might call a "stable" degree of salience, or rhythmic prominence, as opposed to the "snapping/biting" rhythm, which is more "unstable." Also shared between the KMP and the IAP is the important distinction that no stage or profile is considered to be greater or lesser than any other, and—relatedly—no position on the spectrum is ascribed any value judgment either. Rather, each stage, profile, and/ or position along their respective spectrums is considered to simply serve as a means of identifying patterns in musicking, which can then be applied to the session participant's goals and objectives to determine any pathological issues in need of being addressed. For instance, in considering the IAP of salience, there may be some situations that call for a less stable sort of rhythmic prominence in improvisation, perhaps in order to promote a sense of comfort with the unknown or uncertainty, where another session participant or situation might require more stability. It is up to the therapist, in conjunction with their session participants and their established needs and goals, to determine the path forward.

Here is another way to frame the differences between how

MT-BCs and R-DMTs perceive the needs of the individuals they serve: music therapists are listening for body rhythms and processes that are largely *internal* (processed inside our heads, regardless of how or where the sound is produced), whereas dance/movement therapists are looking for body rhythms that are more largely external (produced/processed outside of our heads) as indicators of the internal. Thus, the body serves as a primary source of assessment information in dance/movement therapy, whereas it may function as a contributor to assessment in music therapy, but never in any sort of broad singular way, and always as part of a musical whole.

With this in mind then, we progress in this chapter with the realization that we as music therapists are trained to perceive rhythmic elements differently from dance/movement therapists, and should never seek to make any broad assessments based on our session participants' movements apart from the music. We can certainly consider how external movements may connect to the internal processes at work in our music therapy sessions, and how we might more efficiently recognize and utilize the body as an instrument (Bendel-Rozow, 2018), but venturing to generalize any further about what an individual's posture or movement may say about them in any larger sense outside the music-based interactions we have with them is best left to a registered dance/movement therapist.

The value of personal exploration

As we move forward with the discussion of movement and music in a cultural context, it is important to consider and become comfortable with how our own bodies move as instruments and cultural beings, so that we can facilitate such experiences most effectively (Blanc, 2018; Eckhaus, 2018). This comes from bolstering not only our knowledge of various cultural forms of movement and expression, but honoring our own embodied experience with them. For instance, I come from an ethnically mixed family, but all my living relatives on both parents' sides were born in the Caribbean, so white, Black or otherwise, the Caribbean culture dominates our traditions. Caribbean people love a good party, and dance always features at every family gathering, whether the space appears to have been set up for it or not. In fact, one of my favorite childhood memories of dancing is at a house party where dance broke out in the kitchen, with my grandmother and aunts rhythmically grooving from one appliance to the next, the smell of delicious curry and other spices filling the air.

With this in mind, consider the case example that opened this chapter. Something that might have been valuable for my white co-facilitator to know in the drumming experience described at the opening of this chapter is that any sort of musicking in most African diasporic traditions is heavily tied to movement; thus, drumming and dancing often go hand in hand. Attempting to separate or stifle any one of these two elements limits the whole of the experience. Once this knowledge was shared with my co-facilitator, and space given for participants to move within the music in future sessions, their affect and engagement on the whole improved.

Also important to note here in the exploration of one's own comfort with and intrinsic knowledge of how their body moves is a willingness to be gentle with oneself in this process. Each culture is an iceberg unto itself, and while at any given moment individual elements of stylistic movement may be discernable to outside observers as being unique to an individual or group of people, beneath the surface of these icebergs lie large-scale beliefs about elements such as modesty, gender norms, and societal roles, much of which will be invisible to the outside observer (Hall, 1976). With this in mind, it may be necessary for you to investigate and interrogate any messages or beliefs you may have internalized (whether from within your cultural group or outside it) regarding the vehicle of your body and how it can, should, or does move. This is not to say that you may need to change anything at all, but a healthy awareness of your own sense of physical and internalized self should only serve to strengthen your comfort with being a facilitator of movement-based experiences for yourself and your session participants.

So, as you read on in this chapter about the different forms of cultural movement discussed here, consider investigating where in your community you might find a class to take or videos to engage with in order to become familiar and comfortable with how your own unique body moves through these various forms, *before* you introduce them in the therapeutic relationship. Then, as you introduce movement experiences to session participants, keep in mind each individual's comfort, priorities, needs, and abilities in accordance with their music therapy goals (Grocke & Wigram, 2006). For example, in the drumming experience described earlier, my co-facilitator was acting out of an assumption that an inability to "stay in your seats" while playing was a disruptive behavior, rather than an extension of participants' musical engagement, thus not allowing space for movement was counter-intuitive to those participants in that moment. However, there can also be experiences where the use of movement may be contraindicated, such that it would interfere with client goals relating to comfort or focus in a given area. Participant needs, as always, must be at the center of any movement work.

Cultural forms of movement

I have chosen to organize the following sections into types of movement as follows: fingerplays and action songs, group social dances (circle and line dances, etc.), partner dances, and solo/group "presentation-" style dances (dances intended for an audience). These classifications are based on and influenced by my own sense of how dance and movement are generally shared societally across cultures, from smaller-scale engagement with young children on a one-to-one level to larger-scale familial or celebratory events and/or stage-based venues. Historical folkloric styles and more modern pop styles will be covered in each setting, along with the following:

- A general overview of relevant terminologies and historical context for describing the dance styles as well as any insights from my own personal study, research, or perspectives of dancers I've interacted with, as it relates to dance/culture in the various geographical regions within which I've had experience (or connections to others who have).

- Specific information for how movement may be connected to music we bring into sessions without us realizing it, and how we can be more conscious in doing this in music therapy practice, as well as any resources for you to locate more information.

My focus in doing this will not be on teaching any specifics of these styles, but rather highlighting them in a general sense to bring awareness to how they may be referenced in a musical context. That said, do be aware that some of this information may be supported or contradicted by your own personal experience. We are all individuals, and there's no possible way I could represent all cultures to the fullest extent of their depth and range in this chapter. What I have instead endeavored to do here is to present as much as I can confidently discuss from a place of respect and encouragement for you as a culturally cognizant professional to consider the differing perspectives that participants in your sessions *may* bring from various backgrounds. Additionally, I will highlight a few traditions or customs that I'm aware of in order to point you toward some possible directions for inquiry or exploration into movement experiences that might be most valuable for the individuals you are serving.

Fingerplays and action songs
Overview
Action songs that utilize the body to make beats or tell a story are often some of the first music we can remember learning as children. Note that this is different from the first music you may remember *hearing*, as that can vary. Fingerplays and songs with beat motions like "Itsy Bitsy Spider" (familiar to many individuals raised in America) are passed down generationally, and serve as building blocks for creative expression and explorations (Feierabend, 2003). They can also help to build joint attention, a crucial skill for child development which, over time, will lend itself well to other forms of movement, like circle dances (Shree, 2018).

Guidelines and resources for clinical use
Fingerplays and related action songs can be incredibly useful in integrative experiences that invite fine-motor engagement. Professionals wishing to locate fingerplay songs from around the

world may benefit from visiting the Mama Lisa website,[1] which features children's songs and nursery rhymes from around the world, usually complete with lyrics in both the native language of the song and English translations (or a request for such information if they don't have it). Some songs are even accompanied by audio files. A similar resource in paperback form is John M. Feirabend's (2003) *The Book of Fingerplays and Action Songs*, which is part of a series of texts on songs for children which include sheet music of songs presented in their original language. Similar to the Mama Lisa site, however, not every song has a translation. Both resources tend to heavily favor Western/Eurocentric music. However, with the Mama Lisa site being a living document at least, new material or resources may be uploaded there at any time.

An important note on cultural sensitivity

As an additional consideration, it might also be worth investigating gestures to *avoid* as much as you seek out gestures to *use*. You may well find in conversation with your session participants or others from related cultures that there are gestures that might have a connotation we wouldn't otherwise realize, but definitely wouldn't want to accidentally utilize to cause offense! Examples that come to mind are the solitary middle finger presented with the back of the hand (in American culture), or the first two fingers, also presented with the back of the hand (considered a rude gesture in the UK).

In general, as with most of the guidelines you'll find here, you're encouraged to ask your clients/participants in your sessions (and their loved ones) as much as possible about any songs that may be familiar or meaningful to them, and then follow up with your own research to locate materials you can use to supplement the information you've received.

Group social dances (circles and lines, etc.)
Overview and guidelines

Folkloric dance is defined as dance that is performed within a

---

1   www.mamalisa.com

community by the members of said community for recreational or ritualistic purposes (Folk dance, 2017). From the American and Australian Country Line Dances to the Jewish Hora and beyond, circle and line dances are a cross-cultural phenomenon—every cultural group seems to have them. These dances are not typically intended for an audience, but may be staged, as many often are (we'll discuss staged/performance-based dances later in the chapter). In this section, however, we'll be focusing solely on those dances that are recreational in nature, as some individuals or cultures may not be comfortable doing ritual cultural dances in mixed company, or with someone who is not from their culture. Some dances, like many of those found in indigenous (Native American) communities, are part of traditions that are closed to outsiders. Considering the exploitation that has occurred to some of these marginalized populations, this is understandable! When I find myself encountering a closed tradition, I typically just thank the individual or group who informed me of that fact, and then move on to ask what else I might bring to the musical environment that might be meaningful.

Even in recreational group dance, some cultural groups may have perspectives on gender mixing in dance that are important to keep in mind. I've observed and been informed of rules relating to men and women in Orthodox Ashkenazi Jewish communities, for example, who dance on separate sides of the room (if they do so in each other's presence at all) (Bendel-Rozow, 2018). There may also be issues of touch, as many circle dances involve holding hands, and some women may not be comfortable holding hands with a man in a circle.

Some circle dances in various cultures, like the Dabke (a dance found in many Middle Eastern Muslim cultures) have a designated "leader," someone who cues the rest of the group with movements and travel directions, sometimes turning the circle into a snake like pattern that weaves across a room (Dinicu, 2011). Many Latin American line dances (like the Cumbia, a dance commonly performed at Quinceaneras and other celebrations of life) operate in similar fashions. In these situations, it's valuable to defer to the individual leading the dance, as there may be individual nuances to how their particular cultural group conducts the movements. As an example, a Lebanese Dabke is going to look different from a Palestinian one, even if the rhythm used to accompany them is exactly the same. You may also notice differences between more urban and rural performers of the dance. City folk may present with more rhythmic diversity and fills but smaller ranges of motion, where more rural groups might possibly present less complicated rhythmic variations but with a larger range of movement, more instrument use, and singing (Shree, 2018).

Group social dances may also involve the use of props. Coming up in this section, I'll discuss my own experience as a Caribbean-American with the popular Caribbean dance/game of "Limbo," but another that comes to mind is the Filipino Tingling dance, which involves one or two dancers performing a series of steps and jumps between two bamboo bars that are held parallel to each other and alternately tapped on the ground or tapped together under the dancers' feet. Props, in dances like these, can be a vital part of the musical and cultural tapestry of the tradition.

Resource suggestions

As with any of the dance/movement styles mentioned in this chapter, your best resource is going to be your clients/participants in your sessions. The following questions may help you in ascertaining some names of songs or dances you might find useful for adding to your music library. I've also answered the questions provided from my own experience as a Caribbean-American as an example. From that point, once you've got some answers to questions like these, YouTube is often an excellent resource for tutorials on any of the dance names you may receive.

Group social dance questions

Think back to your experience with rites of passage in your family (births, weddings, funerals, etc.) What are the major dances or songs that are consistently used at rite of passage events in your cultural tradition?

- Who performs these dances (everyone, just the men/women, etc.)? Who gets to watch these dances (do women dance just for women, etc.)?

- What types of physical locations are these dances performed in (any space, or a particular space)?

- What (if any) physical props are used in conjunction with these dances (scarves, canes, chairs, etc.)?

- How would you describe the movements used? Does everyone do the same movements or are there parts/characters to the dance?

- Any favorite artists or arrangements that you prefer over others?

- Anything else I should know?

My experience: The Caribbean Limbo!

One of the most prominent dances that comes to mind in my Caribbean family that appears in some form at every family gathering is the Limbo. These days it is as much a game as it is a dance, but rumor has it that the Limbo has origins in ritual ceremony honoring West African deities. Both men and women perform this dance and get to watch it. The dance is performed in a variety of spaces with the iconic physical prop of the Limbo bar, a long pole that's held between two individuals, initially at about eye level, with participants invited to dance their way underneath it. The primary rule is that no part of the body can touch the bar. The additional rule that makes this dance/game a challenge, however, is that the body cannot bend forward to escape striking the bar. The body can only bend backward (or sideways, which can occasionally be useful for adjusting one's balance).

People use all kinds of motions to contort their body as they try to progress under the bar, usually starting with a gentle squat/stepping motion to get in time with the beat and gradually lower themselves by bending backward until they feel comfortable enough to start progressing forward. Arms sometimes swing or hang behind the body, are placed parallel to the sides, gently resting on the thighs, or they are held out to the sides away from the body. Once the body has successfully cleared the bar they may use the same gentle squat/

step to raise the body back to an upright position, or swing the body around the side and end leaning forward as part of their victory dance (and there's always a little victory dance after clearing the bar!). In the event that the individual doesn't clear the bar, there's usually still some sort of moment for them to slap the floor or find some other way to boogie back their dignity before the next dancer comes along.

After everyone in the group has either gone under the bar successfully or been eliminated (by falling down, striking the bar, or breaking the body-bending rule), then the bar is lowered at an interval determined by the two individuals holding it. Usually the increments are smaller and kinder earlier in the game and then get wider and more challenging as the game goes on. At the end of the game/dance, when only one individual is left who can successfully cross under the bar, that person wins money or some other pre-determined prize. The game/dance can be quite lucrative! In fact, it's not uncommon in my family for people to toss money at dancers as they go under the bar in general, as a form of encouragement and reward for making it through each additional round. This practice of rewarding dancers or individuals of honor by tossing money or pinning it to their clothing is actually something you may see in a number of traditions from the African diaspora. Even today, in places like New Orleans, it's a tradition for people on their birthdays to wear a bobby pin prominently attached to their clothing, with the intention that throughout the day, people will pin money to it. This practice has also been utilized at my family's weddings—the bride and groom get pinned with money (though I also have a childhood memory of someone pinning money to me too as I got down on the dance floor!).

My family's country of origin is St. Vincent and the Caribbean. As such, they have some local music that everyone in the family recognizes and loves to move to. The song we used at my own wedding that got all the Vincentians on the floor was "Jean and Dinah" by the Mighty Sparrow, who's a native of St. Vincent. But my immediate family also has a quirky favorite that's unique to us, which I also utilized at my wedding Limbo: Disney's "Sebastian Party Gras," a concept album of songs by the character Sebastian from the

The Little Mermaid. None of the songs on that album are from the original *The Little Mermaid* movie, but are instead Caribbean songs reimagined by the character of Sebastian, with a minimal little side plot about him trying to throw a party for Ariel's family under the sea. His version of "Limbo Rock" is a particular favorite of mine!

Partner dances

Overview

When most individuals think of partner dance, what they picture is Western European heterosexual couples in each other's arms, gliding across a ballroom floor. Now there is definitely an element of truth to some of this—take, for instance, the Argentine Tango, where the male is expected to invite and lead the female with a strong degree of "machismo," or "manliness" (Toyoda, 2012). But ballroom dance is just one facet of partner dancing, and while it has become more globalized—as have less formal styles like the Polka, or more modern partner dances like the Lindy Hop (the first major dance form to be created by African Americans in the Northern United States) (Wells, 2013)—these often gender-bound concepts of leadership and following may not translate the same way between cultures. What *does* seem to universally translate about partner dancing is its role in the social act of courtship; it is a uniquely physical—and yet socially acceptable, in most cultures—way of "testing out" how one interacts with another, and may bring to the fore questions of agency, power, and sensitivity (Aloff, 2006).

Guidelines and resources

One of the most obvious immediate concerns to consider with partner dancing is that of touch. There are some cultures—Jewish Orthodox traditions, as an example—for which physical contact between men and women is not permitted, or is looked down upon (Eckhaus, 2018). So be sure to inquire into participants' comfort with physical contact before engaging in this type of movement experience. It's also important to consider the possibility that individuals may not be comfortable dancing within the confines of heterosexual gender roles and may wish instead to dance outside this boundary. There is a TED Talk available on YouTube under the title "Liquid Lead Dancing" that explores possible alternatives to cis-heter-male-dominated leading in ballroom dance. For those interested in learning more traditional ballroom styles, a textbook like Moore's (2012) *Ballroom Dancing*, which contains diagrams of steps for major forms like the Waltz and Foxtrot, along with guidelines for music selection (mainly with regard for tempo, etc.) is very useful.

I have used partner dancing (often adapted for use with wheelchairs or other assistive devices) with relative success in care settings for the elderly, largely in a receptive sense, to encourage reminiscence and assist in maintaining gross motor dexterity and endurance as long as possible. It can also be useful in opening the door for increased communication or improvisational self-expression between group members. As with other forms of social dance presented here, you can ask participants in your sessions to provide you with their preferred or remembered songs to dance to, as well as their comfort with various forms and roles. Conducting YouTube searches for performances of various styles may also yield productive results for finding music.

Solo and group "presentation-" style dances (dances intended for an audience)

Here we enter into what is probably the most diverse and complicated form of dance in any culture, and the form you may find yourself least likely to use in a therapeutic setting, unless you're working with a group that wishes to use it for recreational, improvisational, or compositional purposes (which is entirely possible!). As was stated at the beginning of this chapter, there is no possible way I could present for you every existing cultural dance and its therapeutic applications and implications here, but what I will endeavor to provide in this section are some regional overviews of solo or group presentation-style dances that I have either witnessed, or been lucky enough to learn and perform myself, with some collective insights into how they may be useful in a therapeutic setting.

Dances from the African diaspora

African cultural dance (and its descendent forms across the diaspora of countries influenced by the slave trade) may serve tremendous cultural value to participants in sessions, particularly in settings with a large Black American population. Evidence suggests that Black or African American adolescents, for example, are more likely to engage with academic or other information when it is presented to them in a culturally relevant way (Sampson & Garrison-Wade, 2005). West African dance classes are among the easier to find of dance styles from the African continent (and most relevant to descendants of the slave trade), and can be easily paired with drum circle experiences like the one I mentioned in the scenario at the beginning of this chapter. Others may find, however, that beginning with more modern Black cultural dance icons like Michael Jackson, Prince, Beyoncé, and Rihanna, may be a more accessible route for engaging with the unique way the Black community moves. In general, relaxing your hips and moving with the beat (as well as clapping on the two and four of any given measure!) will get you far.

Dances from Asia and the Middle East

Over the last several years, I have been fortunate to be a student of Middle Eastern dance, which often intersects with both African and Asian forms of dance, largely through a unique blend of beautiful cultural exchange, unfortunate stereotypes, and outright exploitation. The history of dance in the Middle East in particular (as well as some parts of Asia) can be difficult to trace because of the way it has been portrayed historically through a Western lens, which often hyper-sexualized the folkloric and social dances it perceived as being solely for the male gaze (which couldn't be further from the truth!). In fact, in many Middle Eastern cultures, certain social dances were only ever meant to be performed by women, for women, as a form of recreation and social education (Dinicu, 2011). Some of this is still the case in some Muslim households (again, indicating the value of asking individuals about their comfort with performing dance styles in mixed company), but many forms of Asian and Middle Eastern dance are now widely performed on stages and in classrooms alike as forms of exercise and aesthetic exploration.

Some solo and group performance styles, like the social dances we've discussed previously in this chapter, will use props, like the Chinese water sleeves, which are long silk extensions sewn into the sleeves of dresses for Chinese cultural dance. Many individuals will be familiar with the use of veils in bellydance, which function with similar aesthetic qualities. Other cultures might use balance props, like the large ceramic jars of Tunisia or bowls in the Uyghur region of China. Some of these practices evolved from practical use, carrying water into a city from wells on the edge of town, for example. Others are purely for aesthetic purposes, but can be strong catalysts for emotional expression and compositional development in the therapeutic relationship.

For music therapists looking to utilize Asian and Middle Eastern dance in therapeutic settings, the book *You Asked Aunt Rocky* by C. Varga Dinicu (2011), which I've referenced a few times in this chapter, is an incredible resource for learning history and some basic overviews of various Middle Eastern cultural dances. Bellydancer Mahin also cultivates a website,[2] which releases valuable information on a daily basis about various forms of bellydance as a performance style, including the occasional instructional video! For those interested in more East Indian styles, Bollywood and Rajastani dance are valuable counterparts to Google (Rajastani is more historical folkloric dance, where Bollywood is a booming modern industry full of dramatic and energetic music for movement). Rhythms worth learning for those dances include Ghoomer (which contains what my friend Ritu calls a very "biting" rhythm), and Gharbha (which she says is more "mixed", Shree, 2018).

One final note on this region of the world: It is possible in exploring forms of dance from the Middle East and Asia that you may come across music that is intended for ritual and prayer/meditation. As was mentioned earlier in this chapter with indigenous Native American dance, some of those traditions are closed and should not be utilized in the therapeutic setting (unless both you and the participant come from that background of course, in which case, proceed with discretion towards the use of spirituality in therapy).

---

2   https://bellydancequickies.com

In general, if ever you see the words "temple" (often associated with Hindu dance) or "prayer" included in the title of a song or dance, avoid its use in clinical settings.

Dances from Europe and North America

Something I frequently tell individuals I work with in multiculturally themed workshops is that every individual has a culture that is unique to them, even if they don't realize it. Often individuals (particularly in the United States) from European backgrounds will say, "I don't have a culture," but I find that once we delve a little deeper, great diversity can be found in European culture as well. Ask an Irish dancer how they like Highland dancing (which originates in Scotland) and their reaction will surely tell you (on a related note, from personal experience—don't ever conflate those two things)!

As with many other forms of dance around the world, some of these solo and group dances emerged from practical everyday actions and rituals, like preparing weapons for a hunt. Others emerged primarily as forms of aesthetic expression, like Ballet did in France, or Flamenco did from the nomadic Roma tribes who traveled from India, merged with the Sephardic Jews around Israel, and then continued across North Africa into Spain (Dinicu, 2011). Yet others are rumored to have emerged as forms of social rebellion, like the dances of Ireland and Scotland, which began as social and competitive dance styles but some say evolved into the straight-armed forms we know today when families were instructed by puritan Catholic priests that it was ungodly to dance with too much abandon in their households—so they learned to dance solely from the waist down, so that to any passers-by it would look as if they were simply standing in place (Gavigan, 2013)! These types of origin stories can be valuable for building rapport and cultural relevance with participants in music therapy sessions, as well as inviting creative exploration in improvisation- and composition-related experiences.

Conclusion

In this chapter, we've explored various movement traditions across the world as they relate to the music that we as music therapists might be bringing into our sessions, often without realizing it. We reviewed how music can serve as a motivator for movement and can support motor functioning, but how we often don't consider movement with any sort of specificity with regard to how we might utilize it in sessions, or how it might be necessary to consider its cultural relevance before doing so. But there is great value in investigating the role that movement can play in therapy, as rooted in cultural experience, in order to be more sensitive to the traditions and experiences of the individuals we serve. My intent in the sharing of these resources and suggestions is that students and clinicians will feel encouraged to explore their own experience and movement traditions, as well as empowered to engage their session participants more meaningfully and authentically as movers and impactors in the musicking experience.

Closing discussion questions

- How might you define your own movement history or how dance and/or movement fit(s) into your cultural identity? Are there forms of movement with which you are more comfortable or have more experience? What personal blockages or boundaries might you have regarding movement that need to be further explored or defined?

- Where might you begin to implement more culturally cognizant movement practices into your clinical work? Identify some areas of strength as well as areas where you may need to do some additional exploration or skill building.

- What are some of the resources available to you for exploring or expanding your own personal history and comfort with movement? How about for the populations with which you work?

References

Aloff, M. (2006). *Dance Anecdotes: Stories from the Worlds of Ballet, Broadway, the Ballroom, and Modern Dance*. New York, NY: Oxford University Press.

American Dance Therapy Association (2018). *General questions*. Retrieved from www.adta.org/faqs.

Ansdell, G. (2002). "Community music therapy & the winds of change." *Voices: A World Forum for Music Therapy*, 2(2). https://doi.org/10.15845/voices. v2i2.83.

Bendel-Rozow, T. Personal communication, 6 Jan. 2018.

Blanc, V. Personal communication, 5 Jan. 2018.

Bruscia, K. E. (2001). "A qualitative approach to analyzing client improvisations." *Music Therapy Perspectives*, 19 (1), 7–21, https://doi.org/10.1093/mtp/19.1.7.

Bruscia, K. E. (2014). *Defining Music Therapy* (third edition). Gilsum, NH: Barcelona Publishers.

Chaiklin, S. & Wengrower, H. (eds) (2009). *The Art and Science of Dance/Movement Therapy: Life is Dance* (pp.33–53). New York, NY: Routledge.

Clark, I. N, Baker, F., Taylor, N. F. (2012) "The effects of live patterned sensory enhancement on group exercise participation and mood in older adults in rehabilitation." *Journal of Music Therapy*, 49(2), 180–204. https://doi-org.proxy.ulib.uits.iu.edu/10.1093/jmt/49.2.180.

Cross, K., Flores, R., Butterfield, J., Blackman, M., & Lee, S. (2012). "The effect of passive listening versus active observation of music and dance performances on memory recognition and mild to moderate depression in cognitively impaired older adults." *Psychological Reports: Mental & Physical Health*, 111(2), 413–423. doi:10.2466/10.02.13.PR0.111.5.413-423

DeBedaut, J. & Wardon, M. (2006). "Motivators for children with severe intellectual disabilities in the self-contained classroom: A movement analysis." *Journal of Music Therapy*, 43(2), 123–135.

Dinicu, C. V. (2011) *You Asked Aunt Rocky: Answers and Advice about Raqs Sharqi and Raqs Shaabi*. Virginia Beach, VA: RDI Publications.

Eckhaus, R. Personal communication, 5 Jan. 2018.

Eschen, J. T. (2002). *Analytical Music Therapy*. Philadelphia, PA: Jessica Kingsley Publishers.

Feierabend, J. (2003). *The Book of Fingerplays and Action Songs*. Chicago, IL: GIA Publications.

Folk dance. (2017). *Funk & Wagnalls New World Encyclopedia*, Vol.1, p. 1. Las Vegas, NV: New World Encyclopedia.

Gavigan, A. (2013) *Why do Irish Dancers have Straight Arms?* Retrieved from www.antoniopacelli.com/community/article/why-do-irish-dancers-have-straight-arms.

Grocke, D. E. & Wigram, T. (2006). *Receptive Methods in Music Therapy: Techniques and Clinical Applications for Music Therapy Clinicians, Educators, and Students*. London, UK: Jessica Kingsley Publishers.

Hadley, S. & Thomas, N. (2018) "Critical humanism in music therapy: Imagining the possibilities." *Music Therapy Perspectives,* 36(2), 168–174. https://doi-org.proxy.ulib.uits.iu.edu/10.1093/mtp/miy015.

Hall, E. (1976). *Beyond Culture.* New York, NY: Doubleday.

Kwake, E. (2007). "Effect of rhythmic auditory stimulation on gait performance in children with spastic cerebral palsy." *Journal of Music Therapy,* 44(3), 198–216.

Loman, S. (2016). "Judith S. Kestenberg's dance/movement therapy legacy: Approaches with Pregnancy, young children, and caregivers." *American Journal of Dance Therapy,* 38, 225–244. doi:10.1007/s10465-016-9218-0.

Longstaff, J. S. (2007). *Typical examples of tension flow rhythms from Kestenberg Movement Profile (KMP).* Retrieved from www.laban-analyses.org/laban_analysis_reviews/laban_analysis_notation/effort_dynamics_eukinetics/Kestenberg_rhythms.htm.

Moore, A. (2012). *Ballroom Dancing* (tenth edition). New York, NY: Routledge.

Sampson, D. & Garrison-Wade, D. F. (2005). "Cultural vibrancy: Exploring the preferences of African American children toward culturally relevant and non-culturally relevant lessons." *Urban Revolution,* 43(2), 279–309. doi:10.1007/s11256-010-0170-x.

Shree, R. Personal communication, 6 Jan. 2018.

Small, C. (1998). *Musicking: The Meanings of Performing and Listening.* Hanover: University Press of New England.

Stahl, J. (2003). "The development of the open/closed movement analysis scale: A pilot study of the effects of different musical styles on freedom of body movement." *American Journal of Dance Therapy,* 25(2), 123–125.

Toyoda, E. (2012). "Japanese perceptions of Argentine tango: Cultural and gender differences." *Studies in Latin American Popular Culture,* 30, 162–179.

Viega, M. (2009). "Body listening as a method of understanding a music program used in the bonny method of guided imagery and music." *Journal of the Association for Music & Imagery,* 12, 21–45. Retrieved from https://search.ebscohost.com/login.aspx?direct=true&db=awh&AN=56602256&site=eds-live.

Wells, C. J. (2013). Lindy hop (dance). Salem Press Encyclopedia. Amenia, NY: Grey House Publishing.

CHAPTER 6

Cultural Humility in Clinical Music Therapy Supervision

Maria Gonsalves Schimpf, MA, MT-BC
Scott Horowitz, MA, MT-BC, LPC, ACS

Defining supervision

Supervision is the foundation of education, training, and ongoing professional development for all music therapists and students. While we have some seminal texts addressing the practice of music therapy supervision (Forinash, 2001; Odell-Miller & Richards, 2009), and an increasing body of literature beginning to explore the various dynamics of supervision in music therapy (Jackson, 2008; Lim & Quant, 2018; Rushing, Gooding, & Westgate, 2018; Silverman, 2014; Swamy, 2011), there appears to be only a small sample from which to draw. For this reason, it is necessary for us to also look outside our own field to those of related disciplines such as psychology (Falender & Shafranske, 2004; Falender, Shafranske, & Falicov, 2014; Stoltenberg & McNeill, 2009), counseling (Bernard & Goodyear, 2014), and marriage and family therapy (Aponte & Carlsen, 2009; Hardy & Bobes, 2016) to examine a much broader perspective on supervision theory and, more specifically, the importance of culturally sensitive supervision.

Falender and Schafranske (2004) define supervision as:

a distinct professional activity in which education and training aimed at developing science-informed practice are facilitated through a collaborative interpersonal process. It involves observation, evaluation, feedback, the facilitation of supervisee self-assessment, and the acquisition of knowledge and skills by instruction, modeling, and mutual problem solving. (p.3)

In her book, *Music Therapy Supervision*, Forinash (2001) writes:

> The focus of the supervision relationship is to address the complexities involved in helping supervisees in their ongoing (and never-ending) development as competent and compassionate professionals. Supervision is a relationship, one in which both supervisor and supervisee actively participate and interact. (p.1)

What is clear from both of these definitions is that supervision involves an interpersonal relationship between the supervisor and supervisee, but also that it is in the service of therapeutic treatment of clients. In this way, supervision can be understood as a triadic relationship in which the supervisee, supervisor, and clients are all stakeholders in that relationship.

As supervisors, we are responsible for supporting our supervisees in their development of the knowledge, skills, and awareness needed to provide the highest possible level of care and music therapy services to their patients, clients, and communities. Simultaneously, a part of this process is to utilize the supervisory relationship to support supervisees in their own personal development, including, arguably, the encouragement and exploration of a multidimensional view of themselves (Hardy & Bobes, 2016). This requires the supervisor's commitment to engagement in their own learning and growth experiences in order to adopt a stance of curiosity and interest, not one of expert. The field of music therapy offers us some guidelines for the education standards which dictate the amount and level of supervision that students must experience in their path to becoming a music therapist (American Music Therapy Association, 2018). However, as a field we do not provide much acknowledgement or guidance in the importance of ongoing professional supervision other than some acknowledgement in the professional competencies (American Music Therapy Association, 2013) and advanced competencies (American Music Therapy Association, 2015; Swamy & Kim, 2019).

Models of supervision

As noted in a recently published article in *Music Therapy Perspectives* by Rushing, Gooding and Westgate (2018), there seems to be a lack of any clear model of music therapy supervision as utilized by internship supervisors. However, if we again look outside our music therapy literature, there are in fact distinct, defined theories and models of supervision. Bernard and Goodyear (2014) identified three main categories of clinical supervision models, psychotherapy-based, developmental, and process (sometimes referred to as integrative).

The first category is those based on psychotherapy theories, including, psychodynamic, humanistic, cognitive-behavioral, systemic, and constructivist. The second category includes developmental models of supervision such as the Integrative Developmental Model (IDM) model of supervision (Stoltenberg & McNeill, 2010) and the Life-Span Model (Rønnestadt & Skovholt, 2003), among others. The third category is identified as process models but in literature is also referred to as integrative models, including the Discrimination Model (Bernard, 1997) and Systems Approach (Holloway, 1995).

Despite the existence of these discrete models of supervision theory, it has been repeatedly acknowledged that most supervisors lack opportunity for specific training in supervision (Falender & Shafranske, 2004; Bernard & Goodyear, 2014). Estrella (2001) cited Bernard and Goodyear's studies in her chapter referencing supervision training as an infrequent occurrence, and problematic, over a decade and a half ago. Even today, many supervisors' approaches to supervision are informed primarily by their own personal experiences in supervision and by their orientations as therapists. While the models referenced here are most certainly useful and applicable resources, we are not fully engaging with effective supervision practice if we do not integrate supervision theory and research into our practice. As this theoretical and research base has grown, there is increasing attention being devoted to culture, multiculturalism, and diversity in supervision (Watkins *et al.*, 2019; Estrada, Frame, & Williams, 2004; Falender *et al.*, 2014; Hardy & Bobes, 2016; Hook *et al.*, 2016).

Supervisory relationships

It is clear from any definition of supervision that it is a relational experience which incorporates the supervisor, supervisee, and clients. While we have previously referenced this as a triadic relationship, within that triad is the important relationship between supervisor and supervisee. This has been referred to as the supervisory relationship or supervisory alliance (Bernard & Goodyear, 2014; Falender & Shafranske, 2004). The time and attention given to the development and maintenance of this supervisory relationship is of utmost importance, and without an effective supervisory relationship, the potential of supervision outcomes is significantly limited. Falender and Shafranske (2004) state, "it is only in the setting of a strong working alliance that the inevitable personal and professional challenges associated with clinical training will be disclosed and supportively addressed" (p.30). Just as in any other relationship we encounter as human beings, the supervisory relationship is influenced by the attitudes, beliefs, knowledge, and skills of both the supervisor and supervisee. Also, as in any effective relationship, it is a partnership in which both parties must be actively engaged and work to maintain effective communication and collaboration. However, one aspect of the supervisory relationship which is present and will be discussed further as it relates to cultural humility later in this chapter is the existence of a power dynamic between supervisor and supervisee (Dileo, 2001; Zetzer, 2016). Zetzer (2016) references Bernard and Goodyear (2014) as well as Falender and Shafranske (2004) in her discussion of the power and privilege dynamics that are inevitable in supervision. She notes not only the dynamic inherent in a relationship with a more senior professional and a trainee but also the other dynamics present—related to race, gender age, and prominence in the field (Zetzer, 2016). This is particularly present in supervision of students, but also exists in the context of professional supervision in which the supervisor is often more experienced than the supervisee.

Also, important to consider within the context of supervision, and the triadic relationship expressed within it, is the guidance of supervisory interventions that comes from reflection on parallel process within supervision. The concept of parallel process emerged in the 1950s, initially labeled reflection, and was intended to reference the unconscious process by which the dynamic between client and therapist is recreated or reflected within the supervisory relationship (Searles, 1955; Falender & Shafranske, 2004). As a concept rooted in psychodynamically or insight-oriented psychotherapy, parallel process often capitalizes on transference and countertransference within supervision. Zetzer states that it is "a key ingredient in multicultural supervision," (p.29). It is, once again, to the field of counseling and psychology that we turn to understand the influence of the intersecting identities expressed within the triadic relationship— by the client, trainee, and supervisor—and how these can assist in the fostering of that which Zetzer references as multicultural competence within our supervisee (p.29). She references two models used to assist in the fostering of multicultural competence: Ladany, Friedlander, and Nelson's (2005) Critical Events Model (CEM) and Ancis and Ladany's (2010) Heuristic Model of Nonoppressive Interpersonal Development (HMNID), both of which note parallel process to be a key ingredient. Additionally, she highlights the consensus that parallel process in supervision is also in play within supervisory relationships, and quotes Zetzer (2016, p.28), stating "This now has become the best-known phenomenon in supervision: perhaps even the signature phenomenon," We will explore this within the case examples later.

Although there are distinct differences between the therapeutic alliance developed to work effectively with clients and the supervisory alliance, there are also many similarities, some of which parallel process highlights by its very nature. A quality supervisory relationship includes a combination of attitudes, behaviors, and practices, such as development of trust, a sense of openness, and a sense of empathy and caring for others within the relationship. Some qualities which have been identified as desirable in supervisors include empathy, warmth and understanding, flexibility, genuineness, a sense of validation or affirmation, approachability, attentiveness, respect for personal integrity, autonomy, and a non-judgmental stance (Falender and Shafranske, 2004). As will be discussed later, it is our belief that a culturally humble supervisor is prepared to not only engage in the development of the supervisory relationship with humility, but also to assist the supervisee in the development of cultural humility within both supervision and their clinical practice.

Cultural competency or cultural humility?

The importance of attending to culture in healthcare practice is exhibited by the multitude of associated terms such as cultural awareness, cultural sensitivity, culturally responsive practice, cultural competence, and cultural humility, to name a few. Although there are overlapping and interrelated ideas within each of these concepts, there are also some distinct differences. For the purpose of narrowing the scope of this chapter, we will primarily focus on two of the most prominent concepts in the literature: cultural competence and cultural humility.

Sue and Sue (2016) utilize a common conceptualization of cultural competence as the development of awareness, knowledge, and skills. This involves awareness of one's own cultural background and the ways it influences personal assumptions, biases, and values; knowledge of different cultures informing varied worldviews; and development of skills to implement culturally sensitive interventions and techniques (Sue, Arrendondo, & McDavis, 1992; Sue & Sue, 2016). As Swamy and Kim (2019, p.221) note, "familiarizing ourselves with the cultural backgrounds, norms, worldviews, gender roles, behaviors, communication styles, and sociopolitical history of different racial or ethnic groups," is central to the development of cultural or multicultural competence. Authors have worked to highlight the importance of these concepts by developing guidelines or standards for multicultural competencies in education, training, research, and practice (Sue *et al.*, 1992). Most prominently, the American Psychological Association published guidelines of cultural competency for psychologists in 2003. These guidelines have served as a foundation for the field of psychology and other related therapy professions.

However, cultural competence is often mistaken for an endpoint, something one can achieve through specific training and clinical experience rather than an ongoing task. In reality, cultural competence is an aspirational goal and it must be acknowledged that no single individual can ever become completely competent or reach a point of mastery (Hook *et al.*, 2016; Sue & Sue, 2016). Due to the limitation of competence being inaccurately viewed as a wholly attainable goal, some authors have introduced the use of additional or supplementary concepts such as cultural humility. Keselman and Awais (2018) explored the application of cultural humility in medical art therapy and identified that "cultural humility has been offered as an alternative, complement and sometimes precursor to cultural competence" (p.77).

Cultural competence has been referred to as "a way of doing," whereas cultural humility is "a way of being" (Sue & Sue, 2016, p.62). The term cultural humility was first coined in a seminal article discussing the training of physicians by Tervalon and Murray-Garcia (1998). Since the introduction of this concept, many authors have worked to better define it and its application within various helping professions such as medicine, nursing, social work, and mental health care (Tormala *et al.*, 2018). Hook and colleagues (2013) define cultural humility simply as "the ability to maintain an interpersonal stance that is other-oriented (or open to the other) in relation to aspects of cultural identity that are most important to the client" (p.354).

As opposed to cultural competence which is more self-oriented, focusing on what the therapist knows or can do, cultural humility positions the client (or supervisee) as expert. In this way, cultural humility can be noted as having both intrapersonal and interpersonal components. Intrapersonal components focus on the need for individuals to have a more accurate view of the self and greater awareness of their limitations. Chang, Simon, and Dong (2012) note that fully engaging in self-reflection and self-critique with a goal of recognizing inherent power dynamics is a key starting point for developing cultural humility. Additional authors describe this "as a lifelong commitment to self-examination and the redress of power imbalances in the client-therapist-supervisor dynamic" (Hook *et al.*, 2016, p.150). Another cornerstone of cultural humility is maintaining an open and aware mindset (Falender *et al.*, 2014). With this type of mindset, one can engage in interpersonal relationships (therapy/supervision) in which one is able to learn from patients (supervisees) and maintain mutually respectful partnerships (Chang *et al.*, 2012). A final crucial element of cultural humility is that it is a life-long process of developing a way of being in the world and in relationships with others and self (Chang *et al.*, 2012; Hook *et al.*, 2016; Tervalon & Murray-Garcia, 1998). While this idea of an ongoing process is present in many of the other concepts of working with culture in therapy, it is truly at the core of cultural humility, and a key reason that many have moved towards this concept in addition to, or instead of, cultural competence.

The term "competency" implies that we are seeking an arrival. And yet in a world of rapidly shifting dynamics (Hardy & Bobes, 2016) and in the critical and ongoing self-reflection required of us as therapists, the objective arrival points may not apply. Even generally agreed-on standards adapt over time as understanding and perceptions evolve (see the National Center on Disability and Journalism website[1]). This means our self-perceptions in addition to our perceptions of our clients and supervisees will continue to be fluid and evolving. We bring a mixture of several contextual variables that give our lives meaning (Hardy & Bobes, 2016) to every human interaction, and, therefore, our worldview is distinctly ours. It shapes the lens through which we view others as well as the lens through which we are viewed. Conceptualizing competencies as ongoing processes with shifting finish lines based on our own personal identity work and where we are relationally, as well as among evolving understandings and perceptions of various identity components (or cultural components of identity), may be a more beneficial starting point.

The focus of this chapter is not how we, as supervisors, might work with socio-cultural identities of supervisees distinct from our own, or how we might guide supervisees in their work with client populations with socio-cultural identities different from theirs. Instead, the focus is on the continual evaluation and re-evaluation of our identities and their influences on our supervision and therapeutic relationships. Swamy and Kim (2019, p.226) highlight this. They state, "examining our own socio-cultural backgrounds routinely will help us…have a clear understanding of culture-related interactions with our supervisees… This should be an ongoing process as our

---

1   https://ncdj.org

socio-cultural beings are continually developing." While later in the chapter we will discuss the use of the concept of "location of self" (LOS) to engage in this self-examination of socio-cultural identity, we first turn to the exploration of the very specific term "cultural humility" as it pertains to music therapy supervision.

Cultural humility in music therapy supervision

Our field of music therapy has been curious about how to better equip ourselves to work with clients with cultural, ethnic, and "diverse" identities or backgrounds different from our own. In their 2016 article, Hadley and Norris discuss the importance of cultural awareness as a first step, stating that "increased awareness enables us to recognize the ways in which oppression influences music therapy spaces and propels us to become more culturally aware, knowledgeable, and skillful music therapists" (p.8). As referenced by Hadley and Norris (2016), there has been a steady increase in the music therapy literature addressing multicultural issues. This has included promotion of cultural awareness and sensitivity in the training process and continuing education of music therapists as a priority. However, we, too, may have inaccurately relegated them to the category of competencies. We run the risk of simplifying culture and becoming prescriptive when doing so.

Recent publications (Kennelly, Baker and Daveson, 2017; Swamy & Kim 2019) within our field regarding diversity and multiculturalism have demonstrated the increasing awareness of the importance of diversity, cultural awareness, and intersectionality. While the field of music therapy seems to be devoting the majority of its attention to the important factors that culture and diversity play in our clinical practice, some authors have begun to write about supervision from a culturally centered perspective. Swamy's (2011) article on culturally centered music therapy supervision references the support of a supervisee in the development of her shifting ethnic identity. Overall, however, the impact of culture and identity within clinical supervision has received limited attention within the field of music therapy. It is immensely important that, as clinical supervisors, we are giving ample attention to how we are speaking about, discussing, modelling, and working with issues of culture and diversity for both our supervisees and the clients they are serving. Research indicates that it is incumbent on the supervisor to broach topics of culture in supervision and this is a part of, dare we say it, supervisor competence (Falender & Shafranske, 2004). And often doing this requires that we have the courage to misstep, accept our limitations, and admit what we do not know (Zetzer, 2016; Swamy & Kim, 2019). "Instead of viewing mistakes or cultural missteps as experiences to avoid, supervisors can benefit by seeing errors as a natural part of the learning process," (Swamy & Kim, 2019, p.223). A case example utilized later in this chapter highlights that "by accepting what we do not know, we open ourselves to learning more, giving ourselves permission to ask questions and challenge our existing approaches," (Swamy & Kim, 2019, p.224). When we, as supervisors, model the acceptance of responsibility for our learning and growth as well as model "having the courage to walk the tightrope by engaging in these necessary conversations," (Watson, 2016, p.62), we de-center our own position to make room for other voices (Swamy & Kim, 2019). Additionally, highlighting the triadic relationship once again, we honor our commitment, simultaneously to both our supervisors and the diverse clients we serve (Watson, 2016).

We can no longer rely on a course or two in training programs, nor the few songs in Spanish or the few associated with ethnic or cultural minority populations we may encounter, to prepare our students to be culturally competent, culturally humble, or even curious. Dedicated, conscious, acute attention to the preparation of culturally sensitive clinicians (Hardy & Bobes, 2016) requires a comprehensive pathway that we are beginning to forge. The supervisor-supervisee relationship is a powerful place in which to do this work given the opportunities inherent in the client–therapist–supervisor dynamic (Hook et. al., 2016). We, as supervisors, can utilize this relationship to explore the cultural self—both our own and those of our supervisees—and promote self-reflection and awareness. This relational work is the context for cultural humility in supervision: "The more comprehensively we can see ourselves and others, the greater the degree of compassion, understanding, and humility we can have for each other" (Hardy & Bobes, 2016, p.6). How do we come to comprehensively see ourselves?

Comprehensively seeing ourselves— locating ourselves in supervision

While, as we've described, our call to action across the last several decades has been to see the "other," doing so in the absence of seeing ourselves is problematic. What is the process by which we come to comprehensively "see" ourselves? Locating ourselves (location of self or LOS) (Jones 2016) is an important place from which to begin, and doing so in supervision is a critical first step. While some music therapists may never before have thought about their multitude of identities, we, as supervisors, can begin to disclose our identity in order to model and support the identity work of our supervisees. Examination and increased awareness of our overlapping identities—racial, ethnic, cultural, marital, parental, socio-economic class, sexual orientation, gender identity, religious/ spiritual status, among others—can help us to understand how the social locations in the room impact our work as supervisors. How do each of our identities hold and express power in our society (Zetzer, 2016)? How do they situate us within socially oppressed groups and socially privileged groups? What are the potential influences of the particular privileged and subjugated identities we hold? Our social locations and relationship comfort, feelings of worth as well as our relationship wounding and distress are linked (Jones, 2016). How do our identities—and our subsequent relational comfort and wounding—inform the information we present?

While there is "growing literature on self-disclosure" (Jones, 2016, p.17), its use within therapy, for many of us, is uncomfortable. Many of us have not been taught the use of self-disclosure as a therapeutic tool and yet if we are modeling disclosing and discussing social location in supervision, it is ultimately in service of its use in therapy. But the personal is always present. Can the deeply personal be integrated into or co-exist with the wholly professional within a multicultural therapeutic or supervisory relationship (Zetzer, 2016)?

Location of self (Maria Gonsalves Schimpf)

My perspective of this work is shaped by my identities. Because they inform what and how I share, locating myself with some of my current and primary identities is important. I am a 40-something, white, first generation Catholic Portuguese-American. I am married to a man and am a mother to three small children, one of whom is intersex. I benefit from white, heterosexual, non-disabled and cisgender privilege (Zetzer, 2016).

Also significant is that it was through the "final hour" support of a friend who identifies as queer and questioned my choice to follow medical professionals' strong advocacy for genital surgery for my third child that I was given permission to make a different decision, canceling his surgery (hours before) and allowing him to remain intersex. I am the child of a working-class single mother who intermittently required the support of government assistance programs during my youth; I am also the child of a working-class immigrant father who I visited on weekends in an entirely Portuguese community. It is a result of my identity work as a therapy supervisor that I now know the ways in which I internalized my mother's shame and her subjugation as a woman. Additionally, my dad's internalized racism as a US citizen—and his quest to assimilate despite preservation of his deep cultural values—confused me as a child and young adult. As his embrace of US conservative culture and rejection of marginalization as well as ideology associated with social justice came into focus for me, so did my commitment to social justice. I am the first generation within my family to earn a college degree. I am a psychodynamically oriented analytical music therapist with multiple graduate degrees. All of these circumstances have been important prompts for self-reflection for me in my conscious attempt to understand where I place myself, knowing that my identities dictate what I see (Hardy & Bobes, 2016).

Location of self (Scott Horowitz)

As noted by my co-author, I too would like to acknowledge that my perspective on this topic of cultural humility in supervision is shaped by my identities. I feel it is therefore very important to locate myself and perhaps most importantly identify the privileges I hold due to many facets of my identities. I am a white, heterosexual, cisgendered, able-bodied male in his late 30s. I am married to a woman and am a father to two children. I am the child of divorced, middle-class parents and, at the age of 26, experienced the loss of my only sibling, a sister, due to a car accident when she was 29 years old. I was raised within the Jewish religion and identify as Jewish; however, I find myself more drawn to the cultural heritage than the traditional religious practices of Judaism. I was born and raised in a suburb of Philadelphia and recognize that both my suburban upbringing and experiences in the city of Philadelphia influenced my worldview from an early age. Additionally, throughout my childhood, my mother hosted international students from around the world who lived with us while they attended a college English-language program. This too had a profound impact on my worldview and awareness of different cultures.

Through my own processes of learning and development around topics of culture, I have been able to recognize that with many of the identities labeled above, I move through my life as a US citizen with a great deal of privilege. These privileges associated with such identities as being white, being male, and being heterosexual have impacted my interpersonal relationships, and the opportunities and advantages that I have received throughout life, including the opportunity to contribute to this book chapter. As someone who attempts to have awareness of their privilege (although certainly imperfect in that endeavor), I find myself at times questioning why I should be the one to speak, write, or hold power in a relationship such as supervision and teaching. It is for this reason that I feel passionately about the concept of cultural humility. As I have learned more about this topic, it provides not only a way for me to understand cultural dynamics in therapy and supervision, but also guidance on a way of being—one in which I can have awareness, openness, curiosity, and learning, while also recognizing that I will continue to make mistakes and missteps from which I can learn if I maintain this practice of humility.

CASE EXAMPLES (MARIA GONSALVES SCHIMPF)

In all of the following examples, names are pseudonyms and patients and supervisees have been annonymized.

CASE EXAMPLE: SUPPORT OF A SUPERVISEE'S IDENTITY WORK

Case example 1a: Pronounce my name as you like (no music)

Naasih is a 24-year-old first-year graduate student under my supervision in an outpatient behavioral health setting for adults. While, by external markers, he appears to be a person of color, within our supervisory space, Naasih has been hesitant to address his cultural identity and his social location, including his race. What he shared in our first supervision session was that he grew up in an urban and diverse community within the US. Additionally, he referenced his social class, noting himself to be the son of parents who went to graduate school and have high-powered careers.

In our co-facilitation of music therapy groups shortly after he began under my supervision, I noticed that clients regularly mispronounced his name and sometimes even asked several times for help pronouncing his name. Generally, Naasih's response was apathetic and he deferred to whatever pronunciation the client had chosen. Additionally, clients, many of whom are Latino, people of color, and/ or from marginalized and oppressed groups, began to ask, "Where are you from?" Naasih typically responded, "I'm from California." Clients appeared unsatisfied. Additionally, he was often unfamiliar with the musical styles of the client population and appeared self-conscious as a result. As we stepped into our second supervision session, I recognized that he was eager to discuss treatment of clients but was not yet prepared to address his social location or the ways in which his identity was influencing the music therapy.

Study questions: Who am I?

1. Why could Naasih's apathy about the pronunciation of his name be significant?

2. Why could Naasih be actively resisting acknowledgement or disclosure of his racial/cultural or ethnic identity in sessions?

3. How could an open discussion about their influence on the therapy be integrated into supervision? How could this occur within a supervision framework that also honors the scope of supervision as distinctly separate from personal therapy?

4. What is my responsibility inherent in my role as a supervisor—and, moreover, as a white-presenting supervisor—to encourage Naasih's identity work? Alternatively, what are the ethical concerns associated with the encouragement of this work on the part of a supervisee who feels vulnerable and ambivalent?

Discussion

In my subsequent supervision with Naasih, I made a conscious decision to lead in and with vulnerability. I attempted to facilitate self-awareness and self-reflection as it relates to intersecting identities within therapy by first clearly and overtly locating myself in our supervision sessions. My hope was that this would invite deeper conversations in our supervision that would eventually transfer to deeper conversations in his work with clients. Jones (2016), in her teaching of location of self within supervision and training, describes how she first asks trainees to locate themselves in terms of race, ethnicity, class, parental status, and, if heterosexual, in terms of sexual orientation. She also highlights the importance of honoring the need some trainees may have to keep invisible identities private if they do not feel comfortable sharing. Given the visibility of race, and yet with awareness of the ways in which I have unearned privilege as a result of my race, I first modeled the ways in which I clinically offer my awareness of my racial and ethnic identities in a therapy session. We began with a very simple contrast between the ways in which I am first received in session with an introduction of myself as "Maria," and the ways in which he is first received in session with an introduction of himself as "Naasih." Together, we reflected on clients' curiosities about my Hispanic name's co-occurrence with my white skin color and how I choose to socially locate myself for patients amid the need for clarity, and how my identities influence therapy.

While it is true, as Watson (2016) writes within her chapter titled "Supervision in Black and White," that "color, even more so than gender, is likely the first observable physical characteristic of a person, particularly in a race-based society such as the United States of America," making race the most "visible and prominent marker of a person's identity" (p.43), I came to learn that there were additional layers of complexity for Naasih in his understanding of his skin color. Over time, and several supervision sessions, Naasih began to socially locate himself. A slow unfolding was required, as it was a painful process of unpacking his responses to clients in order to see himself and his unconscious processes more clearly. I utilized my observations of him within groups, his process notes, and my perception of his openness and willingness in supervision to gauge Naasih's readiness to begin his identity work. Knowing that a strong level of trust and alliance was necessary, I remained curious but was careful and cautious, all the while ready to sit in the discomfort when he was. Additionally, I also maintained awareness of power in my supervisory capacity as a system of checks and balances for myself.

Eventually, Naasih, in supervision, came to identify himself as a male of South Asian descent. He shared that his family of origin is from Trinidad though he is first-generation American. He intentionally diminished his color/race and other intersecting oppressions (Ashton, 2016) in order to maximize his class status, especially in the face of the indentured servitude that brought his ancestors to Trinidad from India. He recognized that he had deeply internalized the class consciousness present within his culture and family of origin. As the process of transformational learning (Hadley and Norris, 2016) unfolded, Naasih began to understand the unconscious way in which he did not want his race to hinder his class. In Hardy and Bobes's (2016) conceptualization, it could be said that Naasih's race was a dimension of his cultural self that was difficult for him to own and embrace in the face of the cultural importance and associated pride of his class status. Eventually, Naasih began to distinguish between those identities that elicited pride and those that elicited shame within him. And he began to notice their influence on and hindrance within the therapeutic process.

Case example 1b: Inshallah

Several months later, in a group music therapy session facilitated by Naasih, and observed by me, Naasih responded, "Inshallah," in response to a withdrawn client's expressed hope that his psychiatric and substance use treatment would be effective. Naasih then, for the first time, selected a song in Arabic for a receptive listening intervention amid a diverse group of multi-racial and multi-ethnic group members. The client referenced here was powerfully and positively affected, and significant rapport building with Naasih began which ultimately changed this client's engagement with his treatment. Nassih created a strong therapeutic alliance with this client and then successfully utilized it—and the client's Muslim identity—across several group and individual sessions.

Study questions

1. What shift occurred in this session for Nassih?

2. How do you interpret the meaning of his choice of a song in Arabic?

3. How could this session be utilized in supervision as an opportunity to explore additional dimensions of Nassih's cultural self?

Discussion

In supervision, I began by noting his use of the term "Inshallah" in the session and my associations with the Spanish and Portuguese equivalents—"ojala" and "oxala"—all meaning "God willing." In the same way that he utilized his identity in the service of the therapy of the client, I utilized my identity in the service of my supervision with Nassih. Suddenly, parallel process (Bernard & Goodyear, 2014) was in play and, eventually, could be explored within our supervisory relationship. Nassih noted that he learned of the client's Muslim identity through a chart review. He acknowledged his desire to assist this client with the utilization of his religious and spiritual resources. Though Nassih felt hesitant to disclose his religion or spiritual identity, an invisible location (Jones, 2016), he shared that he was beginning to recognize the influence of the ways in which his conglomeration of identities and the ways in which they intersect impact his worldview and influence how he is received by others. He acknowledged the power of his use of an Arabic phrase in terms of its impact on the client's openness and willingness to utilize therapy.

Eventually, Naasih, in supervision, came to share his invisible identities, first locating himself within his identity as a Muslim. And eventually, within a supervision session, Naasih brought his sexual orientation, a second invisible location, into the space when reflecting on whether or not visible qualities of his person factored into a transgender patient's draw to working with Naasih as her therapist.

CASE EXAMPLE: THE SHARING OF POWER— BEING SUPERVISED BY THE SUPERVISEE

The redressing of a power imbalance

The following case example is multi-layered and multi-part. There are several highlighted components of this singular superviser–supervisee relationship. This case example is comprised first of a clinical session of which both supervisor and supervisee are a part. What follows are two supervision sessions which punctuate a supervisee's individual session, the content of which is all focused on the same client. Additionally, the case session content is presented somewhat objectively for the purposes of the handbook.

I (Maria Gonsalves Schimpf) was supervising Stephanie, a 28-year-old black, American, Christian, cisgendered female in a heterosexual relationship. Stephanie was raised by a single mom and a white stepdad. She had strong clinical skills in the second year of her graduate program and, in a music therapy group within an adolescent residential treatment facility, often made use of clinical music improvisation. Additionally, she regularly worked individually with patients in the treatment facility.

While at this point in her training Stephanie was often doing her own clinical work independent of me, in this case example, she engaged as a co-therapist in this client-centered (Rogers, 1951) and client-led music psychotherapy group of which I was the primary facilitator. Partway through the group session consisting of five multi-racial and multi-ethnic peers, Keyvon, a 17-year-old African

American male, arrived and sat on the group's periphery. He was in treatment due to suicidality and while he was nearing the completion of his treatment at this facility, his mother had not returned communications from the treatment team and, consequently, his placement was ambiguous. Keyvon appeared ambivalent and uncertain when he entered the music therapy group and abruptly left the group shortly after he arrived; he was absent for five minutes and then returned.

He, once again, sat on the group's periphery, appearing somewhat guarded and ambivalent. Every other group member was very actively engaged in the group process and Keyvon appeared to be assessing the cohesive group dynamic. He remained passive and silent; receptive at best. At the conclusion of an improvised song created entirely by the group members, Keyvon startled us with a question. He asked, "Where'd you get that?" pointing to a djembe across the room and in the hands of a peer. While I responded, "West Music," I also understood that an African American male was asking about the etiology of a West African instrument so I intentionally inquired, "But is that the question you are really asking?" What ensued was a Keyvon-initiated discussion about the imagery on the djembe and its similarity to his family of origin's emblem.

The group members listened in near silence for the first time since the group started, as I prompted Keyvon to share the instrument's name, origins, and function. Additionally, Keyvon referenced the phrase, shared with him by elders in his family, associated with the family emblem and its English translation. There was a sense of pride emanating from Keyvon and I felt relieved that he had been heard in group. Then group members asked me if I'd been to Africa. When I responded that I had, a group member prompted me for exact countries and I was vague, and referenced, "Many."

Though we were nearly out of time, I guided us back into our clinically improvised song, intentionally weaving in the ancestral phrase Keyvon referenced in our discussion of his family emblem, utilizing both its original iteration and his English translation. Stephanie was playing an egg shaker and several other group members were on drums, including congas and djembes. I recognized that as we entered the music, Keyvon's response contradicted what I anticipated. He almost appeared more ambivalent than when he entered the room, despite his deep personal sharing with the group. I then switched to the largest djembe in the room to match the drumming of group members with the hope I would affirm him in my joining the drumming dynamic, on the very instrument that inspired his contributions. His response was almost one of repulsion. He turned his body to the side so that he was no longer facing the group circle and though he was smiling, Keyvon referenced the music as being "disrespectful." In response, a dominant group member responded in an address to me, "You can't do that with his music because they don't use music like we do. It's a tribal thing that isn't like regular music." I heard Stephanie to my left, "Hmmmm…" becoming curious and receiving my eye contact. She responded to the comment made by the group member about "his music," by commenting, "Many of us have had the experience of a change or alteration of parts of ourselves and who we are by others." The group began a dialogue about this concept and we were directed by staff to close the group due to time.

Study questions: Opportunities for reflection as supervisor

1. How might you have interpreted Keyvon's question about the djembe and how does this inform your case conceptualization?

2. How is your case conceptualization shaped by your dominant privileged self and your dominant subjugated self (Hardy, 2016)?

3. As a supervisor with your conglomeration of identities and your social location, what is your understanding of Stephanie's final comment to the group?

4. Given the dimensions of "self" that significantly inform how you think about yourself, would you have integrated Stephanie into the session? If so, more or less than in this example?

5. What cultural dynamics would you have explored in supervision? Which would have been easiest to discuss? And which would have been difficult (Hardy, 2016)?

Self-reflection and supervision 1

I felt depleted, shocked and very uncertain about the group at its close. In our supervisory processing time just following group, Stephanie referenced the alliance Keyvon was building non-verbally with Stephanie across his time in group. She was attuned to his eye contact with her and the timing of his choices to seek her out non-verbally. Stephanie had often acknowledged that, as the only clinician who is a person of color at the facility, she became a refuge for many of the clients of color. I was sure that following up with Keyvon was critical and needed to happen emergently, and I offered Stephanie that role.

As I reflected on my role in the session, I thought about Keyvon's question. I believed I knew this territory as a white therapist undertaking work that was addressing oppression and, as a music psychotherapist, the cultural appropriation inherent in the use of indigenous instruments within music therapy. My ongoing self-consciousness about the use of djembes (or Native American flutes for that matter) somehow felt protective. I felt as though I had been presented with an opportunity to both address the appropriation and elevate Keyvon, whose voice I had been convinced we wouldn't hear. I had the opportunity to remain open to receive his experience and to encourage the group to care. And I considered Keyvon's peers' response to Keyvon's reference to disrespect. It was clear to me that this group member was attempting to align with and "protect" Keyvon. But while I sensed a discordance and a misstep, I hadn't been sure where to take it. And Stephanie did, very aware that many group members were people of color and yet wanting to overtly protect Keyvon by utilizing the use of the djembe in the group to highlight the multitude of ways in which important cultural markers have been culturally appropriated by those within dominant, oppressive cultures.

Study questions: Supervisor's self-reflection

1. Why did I suggest that Stephanie had an individual session with Keyvon?

2. How might you have chosen to follow up post-group session?

3. And how might your choices have been influenced by your social location and conglomeration of identities?

Self-reflection and supervision 2

Following Stephanie's individual session with Keyvon, Stephanie and I stepped into supervision. She was able to share with me that the processing with Keyvon was critical. It was expansive, and had depth that I didn't anticipate. What I heard Stephanie describing to me was the impact of my white silence in the presence of racist words. Stephanie described how Keyvon referenced that he often heard, "I've been to Africa," and how he experienced this as subjugating—as though another conquering occurred with this declaration on the part of white people. Finally, while I had concern about cultural appropriation of the djembe given its place within and relevance to Keyvon's family ancestry, what I did not anticipate was the way in which I appropriated the ancestral phrase of his family emblem, pulling the words and its articulated meaning into a group improvised song. My desperation to pull him in and make him heard honored only my barometer and markers for this, and did not actually acknowledge his need at all—which was related to his deep need to connect to his family of origin and his ancestry. His current family dynamics and the ways in which they contributed to his suicidality, all within the context of his mother's current silence and absence, were part of this. As I reflected, I began to understand how my approach and my insufficient attunement to the cultural dynamics (Zetzer, 2016) had been disempowering. In many ways, I was replicating his interpersonal and socio-political dynamics (Zetzer, 2016, p.32) and while my desire to be inclusive of him was valuable, my approach was wrong. My intent had little worth in the face of its impact. Remaining open to this, and in a place of non-defensiveness, required deep, conscious cultural humility.

Knowing that, as a white therapist, there are limits to my experiences of oppression while simultaneously wanting to provide Keyvon with the assurance that I had understood how racism impacts people of color and that I was an ally in the defeat of and healing from oppression (Jones, 2016), I knew inviting Stephanie to inform me that I may have been encountering blind spots was important. As she continued to share the details of her session with Keyvon, I consciously shifted the power dynamic that is, by design, present in our supervisor–supervisee relationship, opened into my vulnerability, and allowed myself to be guided by my supervisee.

Ultimately, it became clear that I needed to address the rupture with Keyvon. Again, seated in a place of deep cultural humility, I explicitly and directly asked Stephanie to share with me the things she perceived Keyvon as needing to hear from me directly—not for my benefit, but for his. She openly, directly, and compassionately shared with me. In the repair that followed with Keyvon, I experienced no resistance, none of the ambivalence present in group and no palpable resentment. Only connection and rapport. I hypothesized that because Stephanie's session with him came to include the open discussion of manifestations of oppression in therapy, relational processes among us had the opportunity to deepen (Jones, 2016). This meant that his relational processes had shifted as a result of his work with Stephanie, and that this then influenced my relational process with Stephanie, which then influenced his relational process with me. His work with her had been first off, healing, and second, somehow a bridge that allowed him to receive my apology and further decipher his own experiences. I shared my blind spots, my lack of attunement to his needs and his cultural context, and its negative affect on him within the group. Keyvon then asked very explicitly if we could commit to continue to educate others—both people of color and white—within the therapy space.

While Keyvon did discharge to his family soon after our session, it was our hope that his magnified voice in his psychotherapeutic relationships—the triadic relationship that was Keyvon, Stephanie and me—would influence his capacity to be heard in his familial and community relationships, preventing a re-admission and fostering hope, resilience, and self-efficacy.

Study questions: Supervisor as supervisee

1. In what ways were the benevolence of my actions insufficient?

2. In what ways was cultural humility employed? Why was it important?

3. What is required of a supervisory relationship to allow this kind of role reversal/power realignment?

4. When did you misstep within a case that involved a supervisee? How did you resolve it?

Commentary

My need to remain curious, humble, and courageous was obvious and it took mindful focus and attention on my part. As a white supervisor supervising a therapist of color, working with clients of color, I knew I needed to be "open to learning about nuances of racial meaning and experience" to which I couldn't be privy (Jones, 2016, p.22). This absolutely requires relentless cultural humility. Additionally, I had to turn the power and privilege dynamics inherent in the supervisor–supervisee relationship upside down and on their heads. This meant actively seeking Stephanie's perspective as it related to my missteps and remaining open and able to hear them. A rupture in our supervisory alliance could have meant a rupture in the therapeutic alliance with Keyvon. Preserving our alliance meant that I needed to be able to expose my vulnerabilities, and engage in transparency and risk-taking. "Trainees who feel unsafe in the supervisory relationship are unlikely to raise questions about cultural differences between themselves and their clients or supervisors, let alone invite dialogue about differences" (Zetzer, 2016, p.29). Fortunately, Stephanie was willing to allow my vulnerability, allow my mistakes, allow me to "keep her race in the room," as she boldly stated when describing our supervision, and guide and teach me. While we recognized that "those who possess greater degrees of power must also assume greater responsibility in relationships" (Hardy & Bobes, 2016, p.12), Stephanie first allowed me to deliberately initiate a conversation and then accepted a power realignment, receiving an opportunity to supervise the supervisor.

References

American Music Therapy Association. (2013). *Professional Competencies*. Retrieved from www.musictherapy.org/about/competencies.

American Music Therapy Association. (2015). *Advanced Competencies*. Retrieved from www.musictherapy.org/members/advancedcomp.

American Music Therapy Association. (2018). *Standards for Education and Clinical Training*. Retrieved from www.musictherapy.org/members/edctstan.

American Psychological Association. (2003). "Guidelines for multicultural education, training, research, practice, and organizational change for psychologists." *American Psychologist*, 58(5), 377–402.

Ancis, J. R., & Ladany, N. (2010). "A Multicultural Framework for Counselor Supervision." In N. Ladany & L. J. Bradley (eds), *Counselor Supervision* (fourth edition) (pp. 53–94). New York, NY: Routledge.

Aponte, H. J. & Carlsen, J. C. (2009). "An instrument for person-of-the-therapist supervision." *Journal of Marital and Family Therapy*, 35(4), 395–405. doi:10.1111/j.1752-0606.2009.00127.x.

Ashton, D. (2016). "Lessons Learned in Queer-Affirmative Supervision." In K. V. Hardy and T. Bobes (eds), *Culturally Sensitive Supervision and Training: Diverse Perspectives and Practical Applications* (pp.50–56). New York, NY: Routledge.

Bernard, J. M. (1997). "The Discrimination Model." In C. E. Watkins, Jr., *Handbook of Psychotherapy Supervision* (pp.310–327). New York, NY: Wiley.

Bernard, J. M. & Goodyear, R. K. (2014). *Fundamentals of Clinical Supervision* (fifth edition). Boston, MA: Allyn & Bacon.

Chang, E. S., Simon, M., & Dong, X. (2012). "Integrating cultural humility into health care professional education and training." *Advances in Health Sciences Education*, 17(2), 269–278. doi:10.1007/s10459-010-9264-1.

Dileo, C. (2001). "Ethical Issues in Supervision." In M. Forinash (ed.) (2001), *Music Therapy Supervision* (pp.19–38). Gilsum, NH: Barcelona Publishers.

Estrada, D., Frame, M. W., & Williams, C. B. (2004). "Cross-cultural supervision: Guiding the conversation toward race and ethnicity." *Journal of Multicultural Counseling and Development*, 32, 307–319.

Estrella, K. (2001). "Multicultural Approaches to Music Therapy Supervision." In M. Forinash (ed.) (2001), *Music Therapy Supervision* (pp.39–66). Gilsum, NH: Barcelona Publishers.

Falender, C. A. & Shafranske, E. P. (2004). *Clinical Supervision: A Competency-Based Approach*. Washington, DC: American Psychological Association.

Falender, C. A., Shafranske, E. P., & Falicov, C. J. (2014). *Multiculturalism and Diversity in Clinical Supervision: A Competency-Based Approach*. Washington, DC: American Psychological Association.

Forinash, M. (2001). *Music Therapy Supervision*. Gilsum, NH: Barcelona.

Hadley, S. & Norris, M. S. (2016). "Musical multicultural competency in music therapy: The first step." *Music Therapy Perspectives*, 34(2), 129–137. doi:10.1093/mtp/miv045.

Hardy, K. V. (2016). "Toward the Development of a Multicultural Relational Perspective in Training and Supervision." In K. V. Hardy and T. Bobes (eds), *Culturally Sensitive Supervision and Training: Diverse Perspectives and Practical Applications* (pp.3–10). New York, NY: Routledge.

Hardy, K. V. & Bobes, T. (eds) (2016). *Culturally Sensitive Supervision and Training: Diverse Perspectives and Practical Applications*. New York, NY: Routledge.

Holloway, E. (1995). *Clinical Supervision: A Systems Approach*. Thousand Oaks, CA: Sage Publications.

Hook, J. N., Davis, D. E., Owen, J., Worthington, E. L., Jr., & Utsey, S. O. (2013). "Cultural humility: Measuring openness to culturally diverse clients." *Journal of Counseling Psychology*, 60(3), 353–366. doi:10.1037/a0032595.

Hook, J. N., Watkins, C. E., Davis, D. E., Owen, J., Daryl, R. V. T., & Ramos, M. J. (2016). "Cultural humility in psychotherapy supervision." *American Journal of Psychotherapy*, 70(2), 149–166. doi:10.1176/appi.psychotherapy.2016.70.2.149.

Jackson, N. A. (2008). "Professional music therapy supervision: A survey." *Journal of Music Therapy*, 45(2), 195–216. doi:10.1386/smt.2.2.195_7.

Jones, T. D. W. (2016). "Location of Self in Training and Supervision." In K. V. Hardy and T. Bobes (eds), *Culturally Sensitive Supervision and Training: Diverse Perspectives and Practical Applications* (pp.16–24). New York, NY: Routledge.

Kennelly, J. D., Baker, F. A., & Daveson, B. A. (2017). "Professional supervision as storied experience: Narrative analysis findings for Australian-based registered music therapists." *The Journal of Music Therapy*, 54(1), 80–107.

Keselman, M. & Awais, Y. J. (2018). "Exploration of cultural humility in medical art therapy." *Art Therapy*, 35(2), 77–87. doi:10.1080/07421656.2018.1483177.

Ladany, N., Friedlander, M. L., & Nelson, M. L. (2005). *Critical Events in Psychotherapy Supervision: An Interpersonal Approach*. Washington, DC: American Psychological Association. https://doi.org/10.1037/10958-000.

Lim, H. A. & Quant, S. (2018). "Perceptual differences in music therapy clinical supervision: Perspectives of students and supervisors." *Nordic Journal of Music Therapy*, 28(2), 131–150. doi:10.1080/08098131.2018.1528559.

Odell-Miller, H. & Richards, E. (2009). *Supervision of Music Therapy: A Theoretical and Practical Handbook*. New York, NY: Routledge.

Rogers, C. R. (1951). *Client-Centered Therapy, its Current Practice, Implications, and Theory*. Boston, MA: Houghton Mifflin.

Rønnestad, M. H. & Skovholt, T. M. (2003). "The journey of the counselor and therapist: Research findings and perspectives on professional development." *Journal of Career Development*, 30(1), 5–44. doi:10.1177/089484530303000102.

Rushing, J., Gooding, L. F., & Westgate, P. (2018). "What guides internship supervision? A survey of music therapy internship supervisors." *Music Therapy Perspectives*, 37(1), 74–83. doi:10.1093/mtp/miy020.

Searles, H. F. (1955) "The informational value of the supervisor's emotional experience." *Psychiatry*, 18(2), 135–146.

Silverman, M. J. (2014). "A descriptive analysis of supervision in psychiatric music therapy." *Music Therapy Perspectives*, 32(11), 194–200. doi:10.1093/mtp/miu021.

Stoltenberg, C. D. & McNeill, B. W. (2009). *IDM Supervision: An Integrative Developmental Model for Supervising Counselors and Therapists* (third edition). New York, NY: Routledge.

Stoltenberg, C. D. & McNeill, B.W. (2010). *The IDM: A Developmental Approach to Supervising Counselors and Therapists*. San Francisco, CA: Jossey-Bass.

Sue, D. W., Arredondo, P., & McDavis, R. J. (1992). "Multicultural counseling competencies and standards: A call to the profession." *Journal of Counseling & Development*, 70(4), 477–486. doi:10.1002/j.1556-6676.1992.tb01642.x.

Sue, D. W. & Sue, D. (2016). *Counseling the Culturally Diverse: Theory and Practice* (seventh edition). Hoboken, NJ: John Wiley & Sons.

Swamy, S. (2011). "'No, she doesn't seem to know anything about cultural differences!': Culturally centered music therapy supervision." *Music Therapy Perspectives*, 29(2), 133–137. doi:10.1093/mtp/29.2.133.

Swamy, S. & Kim, S. (2019). "Culturally Responsive Academic Supervision." In M. Forinash (ed.), *Music Therapy Supervision* (second edition). Gilsum, NH: Barcelona Publishers.

Tervalon, M. & Murray-García, J. (1998). Cultural humility versus cultural competence: A critical distinction in defining physician training outcomes in multicultural education. *Journal of Health Care for the Poor and Underserved*, 9(2), 117–125. doi:10.1353/hpu.2010.0233.

Tormala, T. T., Patel, S. G., Soukup, E. E., & Clarke, A. V. (2018). "Developing measurable cultural competence and cultural humility: An application of the cultural formulation." *Training and Education in Professional Psychology*, 12(1), 54–61. doi:10.1037/tep0000183.

Watkins, C. E. Jr., Hook, J. N., Mosher, D. K., & Callahan, J. L. (2019). "Humility in clinical supervision: Fundamental, foundational, and transformational." *The Clinical Supervisor*, 38(1), 58. doi:10.1080/07325223.2018.1487355.

Watson, M. F. (2016). "Supervision in Black and White: Navigating Cross-Racial Interactions in the Supervisory Process." In K. V. Hardy & T. Bobes (eds), *Culturally Sensitive Supervision and Training: Diverse Perspectives and Practical Applications* (pp.43–49). New York, NY: Routledge.

Zetzer, H.A. (2016). "Power, Privilege, & Parallel Process in Supervision: Multicultural Feminist Reflections on Practice." In K. Hardy & T. Bobes (eds.) *Culturally Sensitive Supervision and Training: Diverse Perspectives and Practical Applications* (pp.27–34). New York, NY: Routledge.

List of Contributors

Melita Belgrave, PhD, MT-BC
Associate Professor of Music Therapy
Arizona State University

Scott Horowitz, MA, MT-BC, LPC, ACS
Clinical Instructor, Director of Field Education
Drexel University

Seung-A Kim, PhD, LCAT, MT-BC
Associate Professor of Music Therapy
Molloy College

Kamica King, MA, MT-BC
King Creative Arts Expressions, LLC

Leah Oswanski, MA, LPC, MT-BC
Morristown Medical Center

Beth Robinson, MT-BC
Rainbow Music Therapy Services

Maria Gonsalves Schimpf, MA, MT-BC
Denver Health Hospital Authority

Natasha Thomas, PhD, MT-BC
Visiting Assistant Clinical Professor of Music and Arts Technology
Indiana University Purdue University at Indianapolis (IUPUI)

Index